Contents

O9-BHL-739

1

What Is the "Image of God" in Which We Are Created?

Genesis 1:26-31

Purpose of the Lesson

The purpose of this lesson is to help adults define the phrase "image of God" and to find out what being created in this image means for our faith life.

Bible Background

The first chapter of Genesis contains only the first of two distinct Creation stories recorded in our Bible. The second story, found in Genesis 2:2-24, is probably the older of the two stories and deals with the relationship of man and woman as partners and with God.

Genesis 1, however, is a later, more refined work that deals with the creation of the world in a cosmic setting. "In the beginning," God speaks the word and creates the world and all that is in it. Genesis 1 tells us that the God we worship is an awesome, creating God, who creates all things to be good. After the world is set in order with beauty and light, God finally makes humankind to care for this perfect creation. There is a sense of order and purpose from the beginning of "the beginning," all the way to the time of rest for God.

The first story tells us that God is in charge and has the power and inclination to create us as good and integrated parts of the world—created in God's image. Being made in God's image is

not synonymous with being made as God. Rather, "the image of God" carries with it the characteristics of what God is like, how God thinks and feels about creation, how God would act in the world. Of course, we cannot read God's mind, but the Scripture gives us insight into the ways of God. Being created in God's image charges and empowers us to make God's ways our ways.

One distinct way of God is responsible caregiving. Note in the Creation narrative that God pronounced as good all parts of this world. At the last, God created humankind and proclaimed it very good; an excellent creature in a wonderful creation.

In this fashion, humankind is an extension of God's dominion in the world. Ancient Near East practice reflected an understanding of the king as an image of God, ruling on behalf of God. Genesis 1 extends to all of humanity—male and female equally—this representational privilege for "ruling" the non-human creation as God's agents. And humans, made in God's image of love and care, are to care for the world lovingly, rather than to treat it as something less than good.

The charge of "dominion" presumes that humans will have the same enthusiasm and respect for creation as God has. That God creates in a way to share power places on humankind the respon-

sibility to have dominion by also sharing (and certainly by not abusing) power.

Beginning the Lesson

▶ Ask the group members to quickly think of as many things as possible that exist in our world that look like and appear to be the real thing, but are really only likenesses of an actual something. Examples may include paintings, sculptures, photos, computer simulations, play acting, impressionists, or fool's gold.

▶ Write all of the "likenesses" on the chalkboard or a large sheet of paper as persons come up with the ideas. As group members look over the list, ask these questions:

What are some of the qualities of a "likeness" of something that makes it seem close to the real thing?

Have you ever been fooled by something that looks so "real"? How did you come to understand that you have been mistaken?

Did you ever play "make-believe" as a child, or do some other activity in which you tried to be like someone you admired or wanted to imitate for some reason?

What was the object of "make-believe"? Why do we do that as humans?

Developing the Lesson

▶ Explain to group members that the phrase "in the image of God" means a position both of honor and of responsibility in our world.

Words for Bible Times

▶ Refer to "Words for Bible Times" in the study book. Be sure the group members have a clear understanding of the limits of the word *image* as it refers to humans. Use the section to explain that *image* does not mean we are the same being as God, or parts of God, ourselves. Then ask:

What do you think it would have meant for God not to create us in the image of God? Would being created in a non-Godlike image make us indistinguishable from a plant or animal?

When you think of that phrase "image of God," what comes to your mind? Help class members understand the uniqueness of that type of creation and the privileges the Bible gives to us as a result of that special creation

How are we like God? Be prepared to talk about the difference between how we are created and the behavior (sin) that we assume.

Words for Our Time

▶ Discuss with the group more about what "the image of God" means. Ask:

What does God look like? What does God NOT look like? Make a point of giving everyone a chance to express his or her image of God, regardless of whether or it fits with anyone else's.

▶ Tell the group that precisely because there are so many differences of images is reason to believe that God goes beyond a physical description to a spiritual revelation. *Image* refers to the whole person, not just reason or will, for example.

▶ Help class members see that if they themselves were only defined by their appearance, it would be a limited definition. Their lives amount to much more than their physical state. In fact, the physical often gets used in our world to stand in the way of the true understanding of someone. The same goes for God. Discuss these questions:

How is what you look like akin to being created in God's image? what you think? what you feel?

How does your creation in God's image transcend your body? your mind?

How does creation in God's image influence your values? your goals? your dreams? your plans? your relationships?

What does it mean to be a godly person? It means that someone reflects God's holiness and love to the world. When we talk about godliness as a way of seeing ourselves created in God's image, then we recall that the characteristics of God that we desire are not so much a long white beard and a robe, as they are to love and forgive and create within our own lives.

Words for My Life

▶ Talk about responsibilities that seem inherent in who one is. For instance, a child growing up on a farm has a much different set of expectations set in front of him or her than, say, someone who is born into a military family. Beyond chores and tasks, there are expectations about taking on a career, or about moving or staying in one place. Refer also to "Bible Background" above and to "Words for My Life" in the study book. Ask:

Did you, or do you have any responsibilities in your life simply because of the family into which you were born? You may wish to relate any particular things you were called to do simply because you were part of a family.

What are the expectations, or tasks that are given to us because we are created in the image of God?

What place does stewardship have in your life?

How well are you personally making use of the "dominion" of the earth as an image of God?

Would the world be a better or worse place in terms of physically being cared for if you were not here? Explain your answer.

Concluding the Lesson

▶ Give the group members the assignment to "keep your eyes open" in this next week, especially for the rest of the day, and to view God's creation as something for which they are responsible. Suggest that, as they look at the most beautiful and amazing things their world has to show them, they make the silent statement, "Yet, I have been created in the image of God."

Prayer

▶ Ask someone to read Psalm 8 as the closing prayer for the group.

Why Did God Choose Abel and Not Cain?

Genesis 4:1-16

Purpose of the Lesson

The purpose of this lesson is to help adults think about the place sin and violence occupy in our lives.

Bible Background

Cain and Abel's story is an almost primordial piece of our Bible. How long have people been killing one another? Simply look at the first story of the first children of the first inhabitants of the earth. The story is fascinating because God is involved both before and after the murder takes place. The first murder in the world's history is not simply an issue between two people. Yes, Cain killed Abel, but that action signifies a further break in the relationship with God. Actually, it is a further separation of the human being from God, for God almost "bends over backward" to keep a relationship open with Cain.

The story apparently addresses the first worship of God. Cain is described as a tiller of the ground and Abel as a keeper of sheep. "In the course of time" they each brought to God an offering from their labors. There are no clues in the story itself for what to bring to God or how to bring it. At the time of the writing of the story, however, the system of offerings would have been well known to the Hebrews: bring the first fruits, the animal without blemish.

Could it be that Cain has been careless in his selection or neglectful of its excellence? The story does not reveal any motivation for either Cain's choice of offering nor of God's apparent rejection of it. Abel's gift is described in detail. (And with the generally concise narrative of the Bible, this signifies importance!) Cain's offering is not elaborated upon. Some commentators have suggested that this early story attempts to explain the underpinnings of animosity between farmers and herders, but Cain is following the vocation given by God to his father, Adam. We have no reason to suppose that his work is unworthy, but perhaps his offering was.

We can suppose that Cain cared about God's regard for his gift, for we are told of Cain's great disappointment. The story does an excellent job in showing the breadth of human emotions and actions. In what follows, we can see already how far humans have moved away from God, how different from a time when Adam and Eve walked "in the garden at the time of the evening breeze."

God's comment, "If you do well, will you not be accepted?" suggests that Cain had not done well and was being nudged back in the right direction. But his dejection and subsequent anger got the better of him. Cain's hands, used to till the ground and bring his offering to God are used as well to strike his brother. Abel ended up dead, and Cain was banished.

Some persons have tried to nail down the exact location of Cain's banishment: the Land of Nod, east of Eden. However, the word *Nod* in Hebrew means "wandering" and most likely does not refer to a physical place but to a state of being for Cain. Even in this lonely place, Cain bore God's mark of protection.

Beginning the Lesson

▶ Form small groups of three or four persons. Invite them to think and talk about times in their lives when they felt rejected. After discussing the following questions, read or ask a volunteer to read aloud Genesis 4:1-16.

What were the particular circumstances surrounding your feeling of rejection?
Was it just a feeling, or was there an action tied to the rejection?
How did you react to the rejection? How did you feel? What did you do?
Was there any sense of violence in your reaction?

Developing the Lesson

▶ After reviewing the Scripture, have group members say what they believe the themes of this story are. Record those on the chalkboard or large piece of paper. Possible themes include rejection and revenge, sin, murder and violence, punishment, death. Ask:

Do you think God in part was to blame for Cain's murder of Abel? Give your reasons.

Words for Bible Times

▶ Have group members skim this portion of the text in their study book; then review the material. Add information from "Bible Background." Try to help group members understand that God indeed did try to work with Cain to perfect both his offering and his way of approaching the world, with warnings and encouragement. Help them see that the story is meant to show just how quickly and completely we can let sin overwhelm us and bring us to violence or pain. To this end, discuss the following questions:

How do you interpret the question of whether God chose Abel over Cain?
To whom did God show more love, Cain or Abel? Give a reason for your response.
Was Cain's behavior justified in the face of all he experienced? Explain.

▶ Discuss the work of God following the murder of Abel. Ask:

What image comes to you when you read about God's dealings with Cain?
Was Cain's punishment enough for the crime? Should God have dealt with him differently? Explain.
In what way did God show justice, and in what way did God show love to Cain?
What was the hope for Cain?
Does it all seem fair to you? Explain.

Words for Our Time

▶ Review this section in the study book. Ask someone to summarize the section, and give others the chance to add to the summary. Form small groups and have participants answer these questions:

When something you do, make, or say is rejected, is that a rejection of you? Can God disapprove of something you do, say, or believe (or fail to do, say, or believe), without rejecting you? Why or why not?
Is life fair? Do you think it should be fair? Explain.
Do you indeed sometimes look for excuses to sin? Explain.
Is violence ever justified as a reaction to injustice? Why or why not?

▶ Bring participants together and compare notes from the small group discussions. Ask them to talk about any particular conclusions or ideas they might have developed. Then ask:

What is the saddest thing about the entire story of Cain and Abel that is also sad but true about our society and our time in which we live? Possible answers: the breakdown of family love, ease of violence as a natural tendency of humans, willingness to allow sin to take control of our lives.
What is the word of hope that is also a word for us today? Possible answers: God has promised not to desert us; we do have the freedom to choose good instead of evil if we desire.

Words for My Life

▶ Ask the group to read over this section in the study book and then ask:

What are your family's rules concerning violence?
In what areas of your life do you or have you condoned violence as an acceptable response to a situation? Don't forget to include as possible answers: violent movies or TV shows, corporal punishment, violent language.
What is your responsibility to your family, your home, and your community in terms of the use of violence? Help the group see that the story of Cain and Abel is our story whenever we decide that we will resolve our pain through the pain of another.

Concluding the Lesson

▶ You probably will run into very different opinions concerning the use of violence as a faithful response in life. Point out that the purpose of this lesson is to look at those beliefs and to grow and struggle with how we live the Christlike life. Let group members leave asking themselves: Is the way I deal with my world the way Christ would act?

Prayer

▶ Close with this prayer: Our loving God, as you cared for both Cain and Abel, care for us and bring us to lives of justice and compassion; in the name of Jesus Christ our Lord. Amen.

What Is the Sabbath Day, and How Should I Observe It?

Deuteronomy 5:12-15

Purpose of the Lesson

The purpose of the lesson is to help adults understand the sabbath and its role in our lives.

Bible Background

The Israelites had, and the Orthodox Jews still maintain, a very strict observance of the sabbath. For many Jews, keeping the sabbath is second only to the commandment of having no other gods before Yahweh. Strong restrictions are placed on the entire Jewish neighborhood concerning travel, commerce, housework, and even food preparation to ensure that the "idleness of the sabbath" is not violated. These rules apply to everyone—master, spouse, children, servant, slave, even animals.

The observance of the sabbath had a twofold effect. One, the Hebrews were reminded of the need for creative rest, as God had rested at the completion of God's creative work. Deuteronomy offers to the Jews another element: remembering their time of captivity and subsequent freedom from the oppression of Egypt. Observing the sabbath acknowledged the Hebrews' understanding of their special relationship with God. Those who benefited from God's direct intervention and salvation from slavery were obligated to remember that others needed a regular respite from their daily burdens. Thus, the sabbath rest was intended and required for all.

Jesus' life was deeply affected by the sabbath. He would frequently teach in the meeting and prayer houses (synagogues) on the sabbath. Jesus fought with the Pharisees about healing on the sabbath: they considered it an act of work to be avoided, whereas Jesus saw it to be an act of deliverance and redemption for which the sabbath was created. The sabbath was about to begin as Jesus hung on the cross. After he died, there was an urgent attempt to retrieve his body from the cross and lay it in the tomb, where it would await the proper preparation for burial following the sabbath.

In the early days of the Christian observance, the sabbath day shifted from the seventh day to the first day of the week, commemorating the Resurrection. Christian believers gathered for worship, prayer, and the celebration of the Lord's Supper on the "Lord's Day," or Sunday. As the Christian faith spread, Sunday more and more became the "holy day" of the week and has remained so as the prime day of worship and gathering most of the Christian communities of faith.

Beginning the Lesson

▶ Ask the participants to talk about some things that they remember from their childhood about their sabbath activities, including what they were not allowed to do. If you are fortunate to have a wide range of ages and of responses, be sure to highlight the differences between the permitted Sunday activities of one generation to another.

Developing the Lesson

▶ Explain that today's lesson may provide some new and thoughtful approaches for the way in which a day of rest is critical for our life and faith.

Words for Bible Times

▶ Read, or have a group member read aloud the Scripture for today's lesson. Identify it as one of the Ten Commandments that were given to the Israelites during their time in the wilderness after being freed from Egypt. Help them realize that all the commandments would have been unknown to Abraham, Jacob, Joseph, or any of the children of Israel for the first six hundred years of their family. The commandments were necessary to create a new community and people of faith, and the sabbath was one of those key pieces of identity and lifestyle. Then ask participants:

Do you understand why the gift of sabbath was part of the Ten Commandments for the Israelites? Let them refer to this section of the study book if they do not have the answer.

Is it indeed a matter of the Israelites being made for the sabbath, or of the sabbath being made for the Israelites? Why?

What benefits could possibly come to the Israelites for keeping the sabbath? Point out that the sabbath-keeping was not simply for those who were part of the Jewish faith and family, but that everyone, including animals, were restricted from normal activity on the sabbath in the community of Israel.

▶ Discuss the possibility of community building and identity for the Israelites because they kept the sabbath. From individual, to family, to neighborhood, to community, to nation, all of Israel kept the sabbath.

How do Christians keep the sabbath? How is it different from the Hebrew practice?

Is there anything else that Christians do that is as profound and universal as the keeping of the sabbath?

If so, what? What effect does that ritual or practice have on the community?

Words for Our Time

▶ Ask group members to think for a moment about the number one problem families and communities have today. Write the following on the chalkboard or a large piece of paper:

"Families/Communities are too busy."

"Families/Communities seem to be fractured and alienated."

"Members of families/communities don't talk to each other."

Then ask or evaluate:

Do you agree or disagree with the posted statements? Why? Are they close to the problems

identified earlier? If not, how can these problems be solved? One solution: find the time to be with each other without other things getting in the way. Point out that a key word concerning sabbath is the word *rest*. Explain that this assumes that we all are in need of rest, and that we all have a certain level of business and activity that makes rest difficult to have.

▶ Form two groups to talk about what it means to their community (not themselves personally) if it truly were possible to maintain a day of rest and worship on a weekly basis for the entire city or town. Have group members deliberate on these questions during their discussion:

Is there anything that the community seems to be "enslaved by" that would be affected by the ancient practice of sabbath rest?

What advantage would a sabbath have on your family? on your vocational life? on your personal life?

Could an entire, diverse city worship on the same day? Would it make any difference if some worship were in religions or faith traditions other than Christianity? Explain your responses.

Words for My Life

▶ Bring the group back into a large group setting, and take some time to talk about the relationship between rest and holiness. Ask:

When was the last "holy" time in your life in which you felt as though you were in the very presence of God? Even though this is personal, encourage participants to talk about

their experience; it may help others grow in their own courage to do "God talk" and to share their faith.

How many of those times of holiness occurred when you were extremely busy, and how many happened when you were able to stop your regular business and be still for a while and focus on God?

What happens if you do not get your rest? What happens when you do not have holy time? (The answer is the same for both: part of you begins to die.)

▶ Invite someone to read aloud this section in the study book while others follow along. Then ask these questions:

What would it take for you to be able to keep one day of the week as a holy sabbath day?

How much arranging of schedules and nonactivity would you have to do?

Is it worth it? Do you want to? What would you do?

Over the course of your life, how much would you lose and how much would you gain by keeping the sabbath?

What might happen if we begin to expect and invite others to keep the sabbath along with us?

Concluding the Lesson

▶ Once again, read Deuteronomy 5:12-15 to the group. Ask participants to think of this commandment as one that God particularly has given to them.

Prayer

▶ Close by praying together Psalm 108:1-4.

Does God Cause the Events of History?

Ezra 1:1-4

Purpose of the Lesson

The purpose of this lesson is to help adults better understand God's actions in history, even our own history.

Bible Background

The books of Ezra and Nehemiah are believed to have been one book at an earlier time, with most likely Nehemiah being the earlier part of the book. The Book of Ezra is a great book of the Bible. It is the story of the "coming home" of the nation of Israel after captivity in Babylon, and it begins to present a larger worldview of God's work.

The books of Ezra and Nehemiah give us the "rest of the story" following the destruction of the great kingdoms of Israel and Judah. Our Scripture for this lesson is a prime example, as God uses Cyrus to bring Israel home. Notice: Israel did not revolt against Babylon, nor was a second Moses sent to demand their release; a world leader simply granted it. This worldview did not diminish the importance of Israel as the "chosen people," but it did bring them an understanding that God will work as God chooses to work, within or outside of the community.

That work, however, does not always go smoothly. The leaders and the people tried again to build a nation that had God at the center. And what better way to start than by rebuilding the Temple, the central place of worship and identity of the people of God? No sooner had plans begun when "the adversaries of Judah and Benjamin" (presumably "the people of the land" in 4:4) came to offer their help. They reasoned that since they, too, worshiped the same God, they could, and perhaps should, have a stake in building the new Temple. But this was not to be.

"The people of the land" were probably nonobservant Jews or persons who had been colonists of some non-Judaic portion of the greater Assyrian Empire who had been deported from their homes to live in the land vacated by the deported Jews. They had once worshiped foreign gods, and presumably still did, although they claimed to also worship God. This placed them in direct opposition to the goals of Ezra and Nehemiah. The restoration of the Temple was not just rebuilding a worship center. It was symbolic also of the "cleansing" of the Jews; putting off all foreign influences and returning to their ethnic and national purity.

Once rejected, these persons became formidable adversaries, discouraging the builders, agitating and frightening them, and bribing Persian officials to "frustrate their plan" until the end of the reign of King Cyrus. This seventeen-year interruption finally ended in 520 when the prophets Haggai and Zechariah convinced the Jews to resume building. The Temple was completed in 515 B.C. and stood until Herod the Great built a new and larger Temple Mount just before the time of Christ.

Beginning the Lesson

▶ Take a vote (without comments) as to how many persons believe God causes, affects, changes, or directs history. Do not be distracted by the qualifications participants may offer.

Developing the Lesson

▶ Explain that our subject for this session is the very issue the class members voted on and to discuss it requires an honest response.

Words for Bible Times

▶ Invite a member of the class to read Ezra 1:1-4. Provide a commentary for further study, and place the passage in context after the Babylonian Exile. Refer to the "Bible Background" and to this section in the study book. Skim Ezra 4:1-5 to get a glimpse of the opposition to the Jews' plans. Then ask:

Has anyone/everyone heard that Scripture before?
Why would Cyrus, a non-Jewish emperor, bother with the return of the Jews to their homeland?
How did the writer of Ezra explain the actions of Cyrus?
Can you think of any other times in the Scripture in which that same type of intervention by God occurs?
If God used the foreigner Cyrus to help the Jews recreate a purified, nationalistic center, did God also use the foreigners

in the land to frustrate those plans? Explain your answers.

What does this story say about God's will? Possible answer: God intends the best for this world, and for God's people. In the "fullness of time," God's will was that the leaders of this world would act in a way that would bring freedom and hope to the Jews.

Does God act in ways that are even more than "stirring the heart" in the Scripture?

What does it mean to have God "stir" someone's heart? Is it only to influence? Does God take over? Is it irresistible? Is it only a dream of some sort? Explain your answers.

Words for Our Time

▶ Briefly summarizing the examples in this section in the study book that deal with God's stirring of the heart, invite participants to expand the list to include other persons (but not themselves) over the centuries whose lives and directions have changed as a result of God's intervening in their lives. Then discuss these questions:

What makes you believe that those persons you have mentioned received God's intervention?

Why is it that God does not seem to bring about change in lives by much more decisive and powerful ways?

▶ Discuss the role of our free will and our decision-making ability as held in tension with God's will. Invite someone in the group to define the word discernment. Discernment is the ability

and desire to seek the will of God for our lives that is not always evident by just looking at the world itself. Recall the responses to your first question about whether God causes the events of history. then ask:

How does your discernment of God's will influence your notion of God's influence over the events of history?

If we are always persons of free will, what influence does that have over God's power to direct the course of events?

God as Creator shares power. How does that shared power with humankind influence the shaping of life events?

Words for My Life

▶ Form groups of two or three, and ask the groups this question:

Does God, or has God caused a change in the events of your own personal life? Give the groups six or eight minutes to share their stories so that each person can have two or three minutes to tell her or his own account.

▶ Ask each small group to develop a list of all the possible ways that God could work to change someone's life. Invite group members to really use their imaginations, but to stay in the realm of the possible! After five minutes or so, gather the whole group, and ask for someone in each small group to read off its list. The purpose is to get participants to be open to and reflect on the ways in which God may be working in their lives and in the world, forming events

and histories to create a loving and gracious change. Ask these questions:

Is there ever a time when God may choose not to act in your life? Do you ever feel as if you are completely on your own? Explain your response. (Possible reason for a yes answer: We have not taken time to listen and discern the will of God; our decisions may run contrary to what God has in store for us.)

How can we prepare our lives to receive the "stirring of the heart" that comes from God?

How can we teach ourselves to see the activity of God in life events?

Concluding the Lesson

▶ Using Cyrus as the example, invite group members to think for a moment what would have happened had Cyrus said no to God. Next, ask them to think for a moment about what happens when we say no, or decide not to listen to the stirring that God brings to us. More positively, what happens when we do take the courage to say yes?

Prayer

▶ Close with this prayer: Our Loving God, stir us today with your will. Keep our ears and hearts open and ready to receive and act on your leading. Help us change our world into that which pleases you, by using us as your arms and voice; in Christ's name we pray. Amen.

How Does God's Time Relate to Our Time?

Psalm 90

Purpose of the Lesson

The purpose of this lesson is to help adults enjoy an image of God that is "universe-sized," especially in the way God looks at the time of our lives.

Bible Background

Psalm 90 is known as a psalm of lament. It is a psalm that, in part, envisions God as an angry God (90:9: "all our days pass away under your wrath") and the members of the community of faith as those who have a limited lifespan! From the sound of it, this psalm appears to have been written at a time of national pain or struggle, as the kingdom of Israel seemed to suffer under God's affliction. It is attributed to Moses, an indication that the psalm should be understood as a response to the time and condition of exile: no land, no monarchy, no Temple, and no time to rectify all of one's shortcomings. As such, it is very much a corporate psalm, in keeping with Israel's self-understanding as a community, not a collection of individual needs and agenda.

As a community, Israel is called to a new perspective in this psalm. They are confronted with their own transient nature in the face of God's infinitude and magnificence; their own frailty in the face of God's might, their sinfulness in the face of God's grace; their need for repentance in the face of God's mercy, their shortcomings in the face of

God's great lovingkindness. So they pray.

This psalm is part of the worship liturgy of the faith community, probably as a prayer of intercession and confession. It would had to have been used in a time of penitence and not, for instance, at a time of a great festival or celebration. In the midst of their prayers, they touch on a universal theme: "How long, O LORD, before you respond to our cry for help?" In some ways, the psalm reflects Israel's faith understanding with God. In one sense, it speaks of the awe and fear of God and how the people suffer and are afflicted as a way of life before God. On the other hand, it is rich with the understanding of God's constant and sure care. There are phrases such as "dwelling place," and "everlasting to everlasting," which signify God's constancy for God's people.

But God's constancy is not measured by human standards; humankind is not capable of fully understanding such transcendence. While human life is compared to grass that flourishes and withers in just a day, or is bound by the limit of seventy or eighty years, God's "day" could be a "thousand years." So, how long must one wait for God? Until God's moment. God is from "everlasting to everlasting."

Beginning the Lesson

▶ Using the chalkboard or a large piece of paper, provide

chalk or markers, and invite the group members to quickly write down all of the attributes or titles of God that they can think of. When the list is completed, cluster like attributes into categories, such as "God's power" or "God's compassion" or "God's tenderness and gentleness."

Developing the Lesson

▶ State that the psalm for today's lesson offers an understanding of God that was important to the Jews—that of the God of the universe, who is in charge, but whose time is conceived differently from human notions of time.

Words for Bible Times

▶ Invite the group members to listen for the images and feelings of a "universe-sized" God in this psalm. Ask a volunteer to read aloud Psalm 90. Then ask these questions:

What actually does this psalm tell us about God?

What does it imply or state about human beings? about human nature?

Why would the psalmist write such a psalm?

In what way does the use and definition of time help the psalmist describe God more fully? (Possible answer: the time of humans is limited, whereas God is "from everlasting to everlasting." We tend to be impressed with things that last a long time.) Explain that in describing God's "bigness," the psalmist was concerned not only with notions of God's power and ability to influence and change a world or universe but also with a sense of awe at God's incomprehensibly infinite existence. Think about how many eons of time God has existed in comparison to our relatively puny time on earth! By seeing God in such a way, we also are given a very good insight into who we are and our place in this universe that God has created.

What is the purpose for human beings to "count their days"?

What is the use of having a wise heart?

Words for Our Time

▶ Have a member of the group read aloud the first three paragraphs from this section of the study book. Without getting too far off the track in terms of talk about space and time, ask the participants for their reaction to the study of quasars. (Note: quasars are primordial stars that emit tremendous amounts of light from extreme distances from the earth.) Then ask:

Do you agree with the definition of eternity as defined in the study book? Explain your answer.

When you think about the tremendous size of God's creation and universe, how does that make you feel about yourself?

What perspective does the psalm offer on the place and relationship of humankind with God? What does that tell you about your perspective now?

What does it say about God, who has made us along with everything else?

What is your role and place as a "creature," or "creation" of God, and not the creator yourself?

When we humans take our place seriously, how does it change our need to control and be in charge of the world?

Words for My Life

▶ Invite participants to read silently this section from the study book. Form groups of two or three, and ask group members to briefly define the phrases: "quickly," "deadline," "a couple of minutes," "late," "day," "spending time," "just a second," "day that the LORD has made." While still in small groups, ask them these discussion questions:

In the context of Psalm 90,

what should be our approach to the use of time in our lives today?

How do you understand time in terms of waiting for God's response to prayer? What do you do when God seems not to answer or makes you wait longer than you want?

How does a busy world keep us from understanding God?

What types of changes would be necessary in your life in order to take seriously the psalmist's prayer to "count our days"?

What is the most important thing in your life? Do you "spend" your time there?

Concluding the Lesson

▶ Give everyone a small piece of paper on which is written "From everlasting to everlasting you are God." Ask them to carry that paper with them this week and to continue to consider their activities in the context of God's eternity.

Prayer

▶ Use this verse from Psalm 90 to close: "Satisfy us in the morning with your steadfast love, / [O God,] so that we may rejoice and be glad all our days." Amen.

Are Our Lives Predetermined?

Psalm 139:13-18

Purpose of the Lesson

The purpose of this lesson is to help adults answer the question of whether God acts in a way to predetermine our life's direction and outcome.

Bible Background

The Book of Psalms is meant first of all to be a worship book and not a systematic theology textbook. As you read the psalms, you are invited into prayer and devotion. The psalms compel us to worship and perceive God in many different settings, from adoration, to pain, to fear, to despair, to trust and hope.

Psalm 139 comes in the final section of the Book of Psalms, which deals with several general topics, including thanksgiving, deliverance, praise for God's goodness and care, and calls to worship. Specifically, it comes to us in a short series of psalms that talk about God's overshadowing of history. Psalm 137 deals with the destruction of Jerusalem; Psalm 138 is a psalm of victory; and Psalm 139 has often been titled "The Inescapable God." The psalmist considers that God is not simply everywhere, but has created and oversees all that the psalmist is! God is pictured as almost invasive; but for the faithful Jew, perhaps after the time of the exile in Babylon, it was a point of comfort and undergirding care from the God who is beyond our imagination.

While God may be beyond the human being's imagination, the human is well within God's realm of thought and knowing. In these few verses of Psalm 139 the psalmist touches on profound themes: God's intimate and transcendent knowledge, the "ever presence" of God, the excellence of God's creation. Likewise, the psalmist raises some timeless questions: Is my life, day by day, laid out and unchangeable? Is all that I am and all that I will be determined before my birth?

The psalm affirms that the magnificent Creator God has set in motion each day and has woven together the elements of creation into a working tapestry of human and divine will. God is portrayed as a weaver; by this imagery, humans are the threads that make up the fabric, each with our unique color and texture, coparticipants in an ongoing creative process.

Beginning the Lesson

▶ Take two large pieces of paper and markers, or divide a large chalkboard into two sections. Invite two members of the group to write, for the next two minutes, everything that they know will happen to them over the next twenty-four hours. Some of those things may be plans they have or particular things they hope to accomplish, but they are to focus on exactly what they will have done after twenty-four hours is over.

▶ When they have finished creating their list, ask the other participants to look over the list and to mention any activities that the two members may have forgotten. Then ask these questions:

How many of the things on these two lists are absolutely, positively going to happen by this time tomorrow? How do you know? (The answer to the first question is "None, for certain." There are too many variables in any life that make predicting with 100 percent certainty beyond our knowledge. We can make plans, and they usually work out; but just as easily, every plan we have could go awry.)

Developing the Lesson

▶ Ask the group members to develop a clear definition of *predetermination*. Write the completed definition on the chalkboard or large sheet of paper in order to refer to it at a later time.

Words for Bible Times

▶ Form two groups. Ask one group to look carefully at Psalm 139:13-18 and to write down every single statement or reference that describes God. Ask the second group to follow the same process, but instead to write down everything that psalmist wrote that describes human beings. Refer participants to this section in the study book. Give the groups five minutes to accomplish that task. Bring the whole group back to together and have the members report their findings. If you can, write the lists side by side for all to see.

▶ Ask the group to discuss what those very different descriptions of God and humans have to say about both. Use these questions to sustain the discussion:

How does the psalmist see God to be different than humans?

What is the main purpose of this psalm? Is it to describe God and us, or to state that God predetermines our lives? (The answer, based on the Scripture's other references to God and humans, ought to prove that the question of predetermination is only a side issue of this Scripture.)

Having read our Scripture for today, what words would you use to describe the relationship between God and humans? (Possible response: caring, caretaking, creative)

What do you think it means when the psalmist writes "In your book were written all the days that were formed for me"? Does it mean that God has predetermined all that we will do and how we will live? Explain your answer.

Words for Our Time

▶ Ask someone in the group to read this section of the study book. Then discuss the drawbacks of a life that is absolutely predetermined. Discuss the use of the term *purpose* instead of *plan* as a means of talking about

God's intention and will for our lives, but still leaving our own cooperation with God intact. Then ask:

Is the writer literally accurate in those statements about God's preknowledge of our activities?

If there is any way that you are able to change the predetermination of your life, is it then truly predetermination?

Most of us assume that our day will be fairly routine, but some will know the pain of a sudden loss; for example, a spouse went to work and never came home. How do you deal with the fragility of human life? Was that untimely death, illness, or injury part of a plan predetermined by God? Are life's surprising successes part of the grand design? Explain.

Have you discovered God's purpose for your life? That is, have you come to understand God's intention for you, as you have been created? If so, how would you describe that purpose? If you are still searching, how might others help you discern that purpose?

Words for My Life

▶ Ask group members to close their eyes and try to image everyone who has been part of their past and is part of their present life. Next, ask them to erase from that group all of the casual acquaintances that they have made. Next, remove from the imaginary group those persons who have only been involved

with segments or parts of their lives, such as players on a team, or coworkers whom they know only superficially. Finally, remove all the persons from whom they keep secrets. Then ask these questions:

Is there even one person in your life, besides God, who knows you completely?

Consider the one person who knows you best. What percentage of your total life does that person have access to?

▶ Repeat this statement that is found in the study book: "God has made me. In the very making of me, God knows all of me. Even better, God loves me." Then answer these questions:

What feelings and hopes does that statement bring to your life?

How should we live our lives, knowing that God knows us so well?

Concluding the Lesson

▶ Ask the members of the class to consider one way in which they might be able to approach their life differently this coming week as they are reminded that the God who knows them so well has a purpose for their lives, and loves them.

Prayer

▶ Close by rereading Psalm 139:13-18 as a prayer.

What Does the Bible Teach About Wisdom?

Proverbs 9:1-12

Purpose of the Lesson

The purpose of this lesson is to help adults discuss the scriptural definition and expression of *wisdom*.

Bible Background

The first nine chapters of Proverbs deal continually with the issue of wisdom: Who is the wise person? Where is wisdom found? What is wisdom like? The Book of Proverbs was developed in a time in Israel's life in which there was relative peace from warring forces and the nation was well-established with a clear worship life and Temple. In this time of peace, there was an opportunity to expand the people's understanding of living out faithful and happy lives. It is just a bit tough to try to answer the question "How do you live a moral and peaceful life?" when you are trying to fend off invaders or trying to resecure territory.

Although it is subtle, the Book of Proverbs also seems at times to be presenting a worldview that "if you are a good person with high morals, then you will succeed" and also that the opposite correlation is true: those who do not succeed have questionable morals and personal practices. Well-established societies like to teach that way of thinking, for it encourages its members to follow that path.

This wisdom literature reflects the thought processes of the sages of the day, which held a view of a three-tiered concept of humanity. Persons were wise, simple, or foolish. The simple person had not yet heard or learned the precepts of wisdom teaching (Proverbs 8:5-9). He was something like a blank slate on which the sages would imprint their *mashals*, the pithy, brief statements, which, when committed to memory, would form the foundation of the wise person's knowledge. Proverbs 9:7 is an example of the mashal form.

The foolish person was one who had the opportunity to learn of God's wisdom and improve his or her faith and life, but who chose to take another path. The foolish, often referred to also as scoffers, are regarded by the sages with scorn, as Proverbs 9:7-8 suggests. Fools are not just ignorant or negligent of God's law, they are prone to the "seven [things] that are an abomination to [God]: / haughty eyes, a lying tongue, / and hands that shed innocent blood, / a heart that devises wicked plans, / feet that hurry to run to evil, / a lying witness who testifies falsely, / and one who sows discord in a family" (6:16-19).

The wise are those who have heeded God's instruction (9:10-12), and they have gained much more than information. Wisdom becomes a way of living under God's rule and direction in which great benefits of long life and success are received as a result. The wise are also just, a blessing to others, prudent, honest, and generous.

Unfortunately, as we see even in our own society, sometimes the wicked and the immoral are able to succeed and to do rather well, and truly moral persons sometimes are hurt and destroyed in their path. We make a mistake, however, in holding up wisdom and a moral life as the end that we should achieve; it is rather for us to seek to do God's will even in an amoral society and world; for those benefits, though not ready rewards, still give us the ability to live lives with God.

Beginning the Lesson

▶ Ask the class members to name the most wise person they have ever known (not the smartest or wittiest, but wisest—and not themselves). Ask them to explain why they believe that person is the wisest. Finally, ask participants to define *wisdom*. Make sure it is a definition and not simply an example of wisdom.

Developing the Lesson

▶ Tell the group that this session will be devoted to a study of how the Bible expresses and teaches wisdom.

Words for Bible Times

▶ Ask the group members if they can recall anything the Bible says about wisdom. Ask them to discuss how wisdom is related to God (a creation of God, a result of a relationship with God, the expression of God, like the Word).

► Ask someone to read Proverbs 9:1-12 aloud. Ask for other, new observations about wisdom based on the Scripture. Then discuss these questions:

Why does the writer of the Book of Proverbs refer to Wisdom as a feminine personality? After some discussion, be sure to use this portion of the study book to talk about the way in which the Hebrew language makes use of both masculine and feminine qualities that are missing in our English language. You may wish to state that the qualities of Wisdom, like the qualities of God, are not limited to gender (welcoming, caring, creating, and others are neutral qualities).

What is the process, or journey that is necessary for someone to become "wise"?

If it is true that there is nothing about Wisdom in the Scripture that would fall outside of any Christian faith teaching, such as a moral center, or being focused on God, why does the struggle to become wise still remain for us today, so many centuries later?

Words for Our Time

► Ask participants to vote on whether they agree with this statement: "True wisdom cannot be found in this world apart from God." Continue a discussion among the members as to why they agree or do not agree. Use these questions to sustain the discussion:

How is wisdom different from knowledge or common sense?

Should "wisdom" carry any different definition for persons of faith?

Where do you find the greatest amount of "wisdom" in the world today?

What qualities do those wise persons possess?

Does the wisdom those persons have seem to be rooted in the "fear of the Lord" or elsewhere? If elsewhere, where?

Should we expect our wise leaders to have a relationship with God? Some group members may end up talking about the separation of church and state, but try to let them see that the issue is not whether the church should have the power of the selection of leaders in our country, but whether wisdom rooted in God is a quality to be hoped for and expected in our leaders.

Is there wisdom in the leadership of your congregation?

Is it wisdom that is a sacred matter, part of a growing relationship with God?

How much of your church's wisdom is based on other than God's direction?

Since Wisdom is given a feminine quality in Proverbs, would you say the Bible regards wisdom a matter of gender? age? social status? What makes someone wise?

Words for My Life

► Distribute half-sheets of paper to each person in the group. Ask everyone to honestly consider the following questions as you ask them and then to record their own answers privately on the paper to discuss in a few moments:

On a scale of 1 to 10, with 10 being wise and 1 being foolish, how wise do you think you are? (Discourage the easy use of the number 5.)

Are you wiser than you were a year ago? If so, in what ways? If you think not, what might be inhibiting your growth in wisdom?

On a scale of 1 to 10, how wise do you think you'll be before you die?

How do you expect to become wiser (or more foolish!) before you die?

► Form small groups of three and have each group discuss their answers together as they feel comfortable. Then ask them to respond to these questions:

How do you believe your relationship with God will affect your wisdom?

If you have children, how will you "increase their wisdom"?

How would your life, and your family's life, and your community's life be better off because you were a wise person?

Concluding the Lesson

► Invite and encourage the class members to "grow in wisdom" beginning this coming week through a renewed commitment to prayer, Bible study, and learning with other "wisdom seekers."

Prayer

► Pray this prayer in closing: "O Lord, the giver of all wisdom, grant us the wisdom to seek you and to grow in love with you. Bless our journey. Invite us to become wise as we give our lives to you; in Christ's name we pray. Amen."

Did Isaiah (and the Other Prophets) Know Jesus Christ Was Coming?

Isaiah 9:2-7

Purpose of the Lesson

The purpose of this lesson is to help adults understand prophecy, especially as it relates to the coming of Jesus Christ.

Bible Background

For most Christians in twentieth-century Europe and America, this Scripture is so tied to Handel's *Messiah* and Christmas Eve services, that it is hard for us to imagine it as other than Jesus' birth Scripture! It was written close to seven hundred years before the birth of Christ, however, and was originally focused as that message for Israel.

As Isaiah writes the ninth chapter of his book, Israel and Judah are in a time of struggle and trial. The strength and glory of David and Solomon's days have been replaced with a series of corrupt kings, with apostasy, and with a lack of faith among the chosen people. The people and leaders have fallen to worshiping foreign gods and have failed to live up to the commandments and hopes of God. The setting for Isaiah 9 is preexilic; that is, the prophecy was written well before the time of Nebuchadnezzar's overthrow of Jerusalem in 586/7 B.C. and the deportation of the brightest and best of Judah to Babylon. It was a spiritually bleak time, however, as Israel faced numerous international skirmishes: the Syro-Ephraimite

War, in which Syria and Egypt attacked Judah; the conflict with Assyria, in which the Northern Kingdom of Israel fell to Sargon II (721 B.C.); and the ill-fated alliance with Phoenicia, Syria, and Philistia in their revolt against Sargon's son Sennacherib (ca. 705–701). Isaiah's words were meant to offer hope for the future to the nation that found itself pummeled on all sides and in danger of conquest.

Isaiah 9 is one of the first mentions in the Bible of the coming of "messiah-king." This Scripture may have originally been part of the coronation oracle for Hezekiah, with the traditional images and ideals of the Davidic king. The image of a wise, all-powerful, everlasting ruler for the children of Israel must have brought some hope to those who had remained faithful all along, but it was not a widely held hope. Most of the nation waited for some type of reform to come to the country, instead of waiting for God to bring Israel a transformation into the kingdom of God.

Beginning the Lesson

▶ Ask group members to list as many ways as possible that people try to predict the future through some form of fortune telling. (Possible ways could include: horoscope, crystal ball, fortune cookies, palm reading.) Ask what means of anticipating

the future have been successful for them (such as prayer, counsel with respected friends or colleagues). Ask: Why do you think people are so enthralled with finding out the future? Is it a sense of power, or hope, or just curiosity?

Developing the Lesson

▶ Tell class members that you will predict the future: before this session is over, you will discuss prophecy and the coming of Jesus Christ.

Words for Bible Times

▶ Take a few moments and ask the group members to define the word *prophecy*. Have a member of the group read aloud the first two paragraphs from this section of the study book to gain a broader understanding of prophecy that extends beyond "fortune telling." Read aloud Isaiah 9:2-7. Ask participants to look for a few moments at the specifics of what Isaiah is saying to Israel, without tying it to the New Testament truth; then ask these questions:

What is the particular promise of the future that the prophet makes?
Who is the beneficiary of the promise?
Who will make sure that promise is kept?
Is the promise tied to a particular time or place, or just

"sometime and someplace" in the future?

▶ Ask group members to imagine for a moment that they are the people of the kingdoms of Israel (which had been conquered by the Assyrians) and Judah (which was periodically under attack) at the time of Isaiah's pronouncement and then to answer these questions:

What would this promise have meant to you?
Would the idea alone of the future leader of the people of Israel be enough for you to receive hope for today's living?
What does the promise say about God?
What does it say about the people who receive the promise?

▶ Now ask the group members to imagine themselves to be the early Christian church members and to consider these questions:
As you look at a prophecy that is seven hundred years old, what might the prophecy mean to you?
Would it be readily apparent that the prophecy was meant for Jesus? (Remind group members that the prophets knew someone would be coming to fulfill the prophecy; it would be hard to imagine that they knew it would be the Messiah coming seven hundred years later. The prophecy served to bring hope and trust in the past, and fulfillment in God's time.)

Words for Our Time

▶ Write the phrase from the study book on the chalkboard or a large sheet of paper: "Prophecy is the work of communicating God's intention and will for this world, both in the present and in the future." Then ask:

Do you agree with that statement? Give a reason for your answer.
While it is true for our Christian faith that Jesus is the one referred to in the prophecy, why is it that other faiths, such as the Jewish faith, do not recognize Jesus as the Messiah of Isaiah's prophecy?
What is it that brings you to believe that Jesus indeed did fulfill the words of Isaiah? (Possible answers: the tradition of the church, study of the Scripture from the Christian point of view, faith.)
We look "back" at the Old Testament prophecies through New Testament eyes and thus identify Jesus as the Messiah. Understanding Jesus as Messiah is foundational for our faith, but what might happen to our understanding of the Old Testament prophecies if we "Christianize" them?
How do we understand these prophecies as having their own integrity for their time?
How does the situation in the Middle East reflect expectations of promises and prophecies of God? What does that mean, do you think, for the prospect of peace there?

▶ Discuss the importance of faith and the long-standing faith of the Christian church that invites us to see Jesus' life and person as fulfilling not only the prophecies in Isaiah, but many other of the prophecies of the Old Testament.

Words for My Life

▶ Divide group members into teams of three or four. Invite someone to read this section of the study book out loud, and then ask them to discuss these questions in their teams:

In what ways do you believe God will reveal God's purpose and promise to us in our lifetime?
What are the "tests" for prophecy? How do we know what prophecies are of God?
As we preach the gospel and witness to the present truth of Jesus Christ, can we expect God to further reveal things to the community of faith? Explain your response.
How might you be able to receive such revelation in your own life?

▶ Bring the entire group back together, and ask for general observations. Point out that God chose to reveal prophecies to ordinary people, including children and young people. Ask:

Can and will God do the same for perhaps even the life of someone in this classroom? What might that prophecy be?
How can we develop an openness to receive God's word to us?

Concluding the Lesson

▶ Ask those who are willing to make a commitment in the coming week to be in prayer for God's revelation to them to find ways in which God's grace and will might be shown to the world through us.

Prayer

▶ Pray: "Our loving and revealing God, show us your presence and your will for our lives. We thank you for the sweep of history and the prophecy that foretold your Messiah. Help us keep our ears and eyes open to the ways in which you might lead us today. Amen."

How Perfect Do I Need to Be?

Matthew 5:48

Purpose of the Lesson

The purpose of this lesson is to help adults explore the meaning of Jesus' call to the disciples to live lives of perfection, or perfect love.

Bible Background

The Gospel of Matthew is considered by many to be the "most Jewish" of any of the Gospels. More specifically, Matthew appears to have intended his audience to be the Jewish communities of faith, including the Jewish Christians. (This may be contrasted with Luke who appears to address the Gentile communities more than the Jewish.)

As we look at the Sermon on the Mount in Matthew, we find an excellent distillation of Jewish rabbinical teaching by Jesus. He talks about keeping the law, not simply to the letter of the law, but to the intent. Jesus' teaching focuses on keeping the law out of the desire of one's heart, when it was often distorted to merely performing a legal ritual. Keeping God's commandments and precepts is supposed to be a means of freedom, not of enslavement to rules. It was to be a "burden" like the sails or oars on their boats, not like carrying someone's pack a second or third mile.

The references to the second mile, to turning the cheek, to giving up one's cloak, to giving to beggars and borrowers have in common the admonition to consider the interests of others and not only one's self-interest. This starts the disciple on the path to faithful discipleship or, we might say, on the road to perfection.

Notice that prior to his words about perfection, Jesus talks about forgiveness and love of enemies. There was a strong distinction made then in Jewish moral teaching between a neighbor and an "enemy," as well as to limits of forgiveness required of a faithful Jew.

Leviticus 18:19 commands the love of neighbor, but defines "neighbor" as one's kin or fellow Israelite. (Now we better understand why, in the prelude to the parable of the good Samaritan, the lawyer asked, "who is my neighbor?") While the law did not specifically state that one could or should hate his enemy, passages such Psalm 5:5 ("[God] hates all evildoers") imply that harboring hatred against "outsiders" was sanctioned.

Jesus calls the listeners to the heart of the matter, that is, who should I love, why should I love, and how should I love? The "who" Jesus extends to humankind in general, as well as to the despised occupying Roman forces. Always there is a local and a universal dimension to the way one should love. The "why" is provided in verse 45: "so that you may be children of your Father in heaven." As for "how," Jesus points to the way God loves: perfectly.

It is important to realize that most of our culture's understanding of *perfection* arises out of our ties to the Greek worldview.

Greek philosophers talked about perfection as an ideal or image that existed only in a supreme being and was a type for all other physical manifestations, themselves less than perfect. Perfection in one's physical life was an unattainable dream.

This is drastically different from the Jewish worldview that understood *perfection* not as an ideal, but as a sense of completeness, or fulfillment of all that was necessary. To be perfect as God is perfect is to have as one's goal the same single-minded devotion for others as God has for us, and in so doing, to serve God wholeheartedly. In our reading of Scripture, especially Matthew, it is good to realize this worldview more closely matches the Jewish thought than the Greek idea.

Beginning the Lesson

▶ As a group, define the word *perfection*. You may come up with terms such as *without a mistake, nothing lacking, absolutely right*. It is also possible to use the terms *whole* or *complete*. Ask them to think about things that they have experienced as "perfect" in their lives. You may mention a "perfect 10" or a "perfect sunset." Then ask:

Is the idea of perfection troublesome? Explain.

Developing the Lesson

▶ Tell group members that you are going to look at perfection from Jesus' point of view, and from the perspective of your relationships with God and others.

Words for Bible Times

▶ Ask someone to write the text of Matthew 5:48 on the chalkboard or a large piece of paper, so it is in view throughout the session.

▶ Ask for class members' first reaction to the verse. You can expect comments like: "Nobody can be perfect except for God!" Then ask the question:

If no one but God can be perfect, why did Jesus call the disciples and others who were listening to him on the Mount to such a high standard of living?

▶ Invite someone to read this section of the study book aloud beginning with the paragraph "Jesus uses the word 'therefore. . . .' " Then discuss these questions:

What difference does it make to talk about perfection in terms of unlimited love and with no expectation of return rather than in terms of attainment (being without error) or of process (doing something exactly right)?

How do the Scripture and the commentary on it explain perfect love?

What illumination to you receive when you think of perfection as a dynamic relationship with God and with others rather than a state we achieve?

Would it have been fair, do you think, for Jesus to demand of the disciples to have that static perfection?

Was it fair for him to expect them to love with a love that

approaches God's love for them? Explain your answers.

Words for Our Time

▶ Invite group members to consider themselves as disciples called to love others perfectly (which they, in fact, are). Discuss these questions:

Is Jesus' talk about an ideal of perfect love, an achievable goal for the listeners in the Gospel, or for us?

What makes it so scary for us to think about living and loving "perfectly" in our world today?

If the goal of perfect love is not our goal, what as the followers of Christ do we consider to be "good enough"?

▶ Form small groups of three or four persons, and ask each group to talk with each other about someone they know or have met (not just know about, like Mother Teresa) who they believe even comes close to perfect love in their lives. After a few minutes of discussion, ask group members to compare their observations.

▶ Then ask the small group members to think and talk about any time in which they felt they were able to respond in love perfectly (wholeheartedly). Ask them to think for a moment, then say:

Imagine you were able to "love perfectly" only one time a year — that is, to love someone with your whole heart's intention, just for a moment. . . . Now imagine, you were able to do that only once a month. . . . Think if you were able to do that only once a week, . . . and then only once a day. . . .

Ask: How does your spiritual growth and life affect your ability to be able to love perfectly?

Words for My Life

▶ Write the words "Journey Toward Perfection" on the chalkboard or on poster paper. Next to it, write "Journey Toward Pretty Good," and then "Journey to Evil." Ask the group members to think about which journey they are on and what is required for each journey in terms of their commitment to Jesus Christ. Ask the group:

What can we expect of God when we intend to live our lives journeying toward perfect love in Christ?

What changes would have to occur in our lives for the journey to be successful?

How might our world be changed by our journey?

Concluding the Lesson

▶ Give participants the assignment to focus this next week on the idea of *perfection* not as a completed, static work, but as a relationship of growth and love in God through Jesus Christ.

Prayer

▶ Pray together: "Use us and lead us, O God, on the journey toward love for you and for our world. Give us the strength, the humility, and the grace to grow into the very likeness of Christ as we become perfect in our love; in Christ's name. Amen."

What Is the Sin That Can Never Be Forgiven?
Matthew 12:31-32

Purpose of the Lesson

The purpose of this lesson is to help adults understand blasphemy in terms of our relationship with the Holy Spirit.

Bible Background

For the main part, the Gospels were written to affirm and to strengthen the faith of the followers of Jesus Christ and not primarily to convert. That is, the Gospels would have been copied and distributed to the Christian congregations in order to firm up their understanding of the life, ministry, death and resurrection of Jesus. They were not handed out as tracts on the street. That evangelizing task was the work of the witnesses to the faith, and it happened by word of mouth.

The Gospels, then, are effective in showing the errors of those who lived at the time of Christ and yet did not realize he was the Son of God. They are also helpful in letting the community know what the appropriate approach might be to the questions that would come to the faithful. In our story for today, the early Christians would have received both assurance and warning concerning blasphemy: hold on to the faith, despite what others might say about the miracles of Jesus. If they reject the presence and work of the Holy Spirit, they can expect an eternal judgment and separation from God.

This teaching comes as a lesson to the early Christians in terms of a story of an encounter between Jesus and the Pharisees. The Pharisees in this setting represent the kingdom of Satan. They had challenged Jesus' healing of a man who, for his day, was severely handicapped. The man was blind, unable to speak, and suffering from some kind of emotional or psychological illness (a "demoniac"). The crowd who witnessed this event was astonished and speculated that Jesus might be the Messiah ("the Son of David").

In a swift countermove, the Pharisees attempted to put Jesus in league with the devil. Jesus charged just the reverse to be true. If he undermined the evil work of Satan by the power of Satan, he would in effect render himself powerless. "But" he continued, "if it is by the Spirit of God that I cast out demons, then the kingdom of God has come to you.... Whoever is not with me is against me, and whoever does not gather with me scatters" (12:28, 30). The implication was clear that the Pharisees were "scattering." They were accusing the Holy Spirit of evil.

Why did Jesus choose the Holy Spirit to defend? We can consider that for most persons in the time of the early church, belief in God as the Creator would be fairly universal; belief in Jesus Christ, and in Christ's power to forgive sin is at the root of the Christian faith. To reject or deny that would mean you were not a Christian. To deny the work and power of the Holy Spirit, however, would be to say that God was not present and working in the world in this area or this way. It would turn the Christian faith into a worship of something that happened in the past, instead of something that continued into the very present with the person of the Holy Spirit indwelling in the followers of Christ.

Matthew's pronouncement here in singling out the Pharisees is to warn the early church that those who block the way to the Kingdom and thus represent Satan's work, are destined for judgment and condemnation. Rather than creating reasons for anxiety for the new church, this warning offers direction for the way to righteousness.

Beginning the Lesson

▶ Ask group members to call out as many types of sins as they can think of in the next sixty seconds. You may wish to commend them on their knowledge of sin after time is up. Tell them that most of the things they just mentioned are "transgressions." Offer this definition of *sin*: Sin is the intentional separation of our lives from God and one another. Transgressions become the expressions of that fundamental separation.

Developing the Lesson

▶ Ask group members to keep the definition of sin in mind as you look at *blasphemy* in today's lesson.

Words for Bible Times

▶ Using a chalkboard or a large piece of paper to write their responses on, ask the participants to think of some qualities of God. (Possible answers could be: loving, caring, forgiving, righteous, all-powerful.) You will return to this list in a few moments.

▶ Give the group members time to read this section of the study book silently. Add information from the "Bible Background," and have on hand a commentary for more complete interpretation. Then read the Scripture for today, including Matthew 12:22-32 in order to develop the context for Jesus' statement. Ask these questions:

How would you define the phrase "blasphemy against the Holy Spirit"?

Does the sin of blasphemy have more to do with a pattern of life decisions than with a particular moment of sin? Explain.

Look again at the qualities of God you listed. Do you think God would absolutely fail to forgive someone for one moment or one expression of unbelief or denial of God's Holy Spirit? Explain your reasons.

How do you think God would respond to someone who, throughout the course of his or her life, denied God and the work and presence of the Holy Spirit, and in fact, did all in his or her power to speak against God's grace and power?

Words for Our Time

▶ Review this section in the study book. Ask group members to describe who the Holy Spirit is and what the Spirit does. Then pose these questions:

Are we, by and large, a spiritual people? That is, do you think most people believe in a spiritual presence in this world? Why or why not?

Does "blasphemy of the Holy Spirit" happen today? If so, in what ways?

Do you believe the Holy Spirit of God is more respected or less respected now than in times past? Why?

▶ Ask the group to identify the last time in which the presence and work of the Holy Spirit was held up in a positive light in some form of the public media. Then ask:

Why is it so difficult for us to hold up and point out the signs of God's presence and action in our world?

In what ways should and could our church support and proclaim the work of the Holy Spirit in this world?

Persons who consider themselves charismatic or pentecostal rely a great deal on signs and activity of the Spirit. Is this the only spiritual or religious road to the work of the spirit? Explain.

Words for My Life

▶ Ask the group to identify the difference between blasphemy and a questioning faith. Form groups of three or four, and then ask those who feel comfortable to discuss these questions. After the small group discussions, bring everyone together to compare comments.

Can you recall a time when you were not sure if some event or belief was the work of good or of evil? What was that like?

Can you recall a time in which you felt God was far away, or set apart? Would you call that a faithful time?

Have there ever been times when you have wondered about the existence and power of God at work in this world?

Would you identify that moment of wonder as blasphemy? as a time of growing and stretching your faith? Explain your answers.

Concluding the Lesson

▶ Remind group members that, as the followers of Christ, our task is to proclaim the good news of Jesus Christ in as many ways as we can. When the world says, "There is no God," or acts that way, our affirmation, "Here is the work of God," is a strong and loving response.

Prayer

▶ Invite anyone who wishes to close the session with a prayer to the Holy Spirit for guidance and for Christian growth.

Did God Forsake Jesus on the Cross?

Mark 15:33-37

Purpose of the Lesson

The purpose of this lesson is to help adults gain new insights into one of the seven last words of Christ.

Bible Background

It is interesting that the four Gospels tell different specifics about the last hours of Jesus' life. Of the so-called "seven last words of Christ," three of them are found in John's Gospel, three in Luke, and Mark and Matthew share the same word that is today's lesson. Why such a difference? It must have depended on the eyewitnesses and sources that the Gospel writers used to develop the four stories of Jesus. Even for something as significant for our faith as the crucifixion of Jesus, the specifics only became significant after the Resurrection and the establishment of the new faith.

Our faith is flooded in such a way with the symbol of the cross that it is hard to imagine it as a method of execution. Yet the method was very effective. As described in the study book, it was a matter of slow asphyxiation, as the person being executed had to push up on his legs for long periods in order to allow his rib cage to expand with air. The soldiers' order at Jesus' execution to break the legs of the prisoners was commanded so that the criminals would suffocate more quickly and be dead before sundown, the beginning of the sab-

bath. Jesus' legs were not broken, because he was already dead.

Crucifixion was the most public humiliation possible. The one being executed would be teased and cursed and treated horribly while he was dying. It makes sense that Jesus would have used the word *forsake*. His entire world seemed to collapse.

The traditional site of the execution of Jesus in Jerusalem is now found within the boundaries of the walls of the Old City. A large plaza and a church occupy the space of both the hill of Golgotha and the area below Golgotha where the tombs were carved out of limestone. During Jesus' times, however, it would have been a bleak and ugly place.

Beginning the Lesson

▶ Ask the members of the group to pair off and to discuss the following question: When was the time in your life, either as a child or as an adult, you felt the most alone?

Developing the Lesson

▶ Tell group members that they will be peering into the loneliest and most agonizing time of Jesus' life, and looking for hope there.

Words for Bible Times

▶ Use the "Bible Background" and this section of the study

book to talk about crucifixion. Help participants realize, if they do not already, that crucifixion took a long time—for Jesus, it took six hours, and that was after he had been beaten and whipped. But it could have taken as long as twenty-fours hours or more. Criminals who did not die sooner from asphyxiation would die later from exposure and loss of blood. Ask group members to try to imagine not only the physical pain, but also the mental and emotional burden of Jesus' execution.

▶ Read Mark 15:33-37. Make sure everyone has heard of and become familiar with Jesus' words on the cross. Ask for their first reactions, or what they have heard in the past about this word of Jesus. Do they believe that God did forsake Jesus?

▶ Invite someone to read all of Psalm 22 aloud. After the reading, help participants see the similarity in the psalm and Jesus' words. Then ask:

Do you believe it is possible that this psalm is what Jesus quoted?
What would that mean about Jesus if indeed he did use this psalm in his time of pain and loneliness and fear?
As you study this psalm, does it change in any way your understanding of Jesus' dying? (Possible answer: instead of a time of fear and despair, it was for Jesus a time of hope and faith that God indeed would not forsake him.)

Words for Our Time

▶ Ask group members to think back to the discussion they had at the beginning of the session about a time when they felt alone. Then ask them:

What did you do when you were feeling so alone?

What is a natural reaction to those feelings? (Possible answers: try to find comfort, or a sense of perspective, to get away from the loneliness.)

Have you ever quoted Scripture (or a hymn based on Scripture) to help you through a difficult time?

If so, what Scripture did you use? How did it help?

As Jesus hung on the cross, what might he have done to lessen his sense of fear or loneliness?

Would quoting Psalm 22 have been helpful for him, do you think? Why?

▶ Ask group members to discuss for a little while the importance of learning and knowing portions of Scripture or worship prayers. Then ask:

Is there any value in those types of traditions?

How well are we teaching such things to a new generation of people who are more visually oriented than orally oriented?

▶ Have participants name or recite portions of "holy words" that have been, or could be, a strength or comfort to them.

Write them on the chalkboard or poster paper so that you may refer to them. During the discussion you may wish to note the importance of using the worship bulletin as a means of teaching prayers and responses to persons who may not know them before they come to your worship. See this section in the study book. Now discuss these questions:

How do you think persons who are "unchurched" or are without a foundation of faith find strength in times of death or illness or fear?

What can we as the church do to strengthen the hope of all of our community?

Words for My Life

▶ Say this to the group: "Jesus' death on the cross was no less painful and humiliating, and no less deadly because he knew the words to Psalm 22. What value, then, do you think the words had for him? Did hope help him die more easily, do you think? Why did he need to speak at all?"

▶ Ask someone to read this section of the study book out loud. Then form small groups of three, and ask the group members to talk about any time in their own life when the most they could pray to God was a "sigh too deep for words." Ask them to consider these questions as they talk about their own experience:

In your own time of trouble, what would it mean to know that God knew what you were going through and was there to offer God's presence to you?

Is it true that any words, even the old words of traditional psalms and prayers, are enough to share our struggle with God?

What is the role of having an open heart and soul to God as we quote those pieces of Scripture?

What does it say about God if we take seriously God's ability to hear and care for us even when we cannot say the words?

Did God forsake Jesus on the cross, do you think? Does God forsake anyone? Explain.

Concluding the Lesson

▶ Invite the group members to read Scripture, including Mark 15:33-37 and Psalm 22, this week in order to discover new portions of Scripture to help them discern God's presence and strength now or at some time in the future.

Prayer

▶ Pray, using Psalm 22:9-11: O God, "it was you who took me from the womb; / you kept me safe on my mother's breast. / On you I was cast from my birth, / and since my mother bore me you have been my God. / Do not be far from me, / for trouble is near / and there is no one to help." Amen.

What Happened in the Transfiguration of Jesus?

Luke 9:28-36

Purpose of the Lesson

The purpose of this lesson is to help adults see the mysterious side of God and God's presence in our lives.

Bible Background

How does the Bible describe God? God's presence is found in a burning bush; in a pillar of smoke and fire; in a cloud that fills the tabernacle; as the sound of sheer silence (or a still small voice); and in many other, non-specific, almost unexplainable ways. Apparently, the precise words for describing God are not in our vocabulary. Yet, even in this list, there are similarities in description: there is a brightness, an intensity, a cloudiness, something that absolutely grabs your attention and just does not look like anything else.

The Transfiguration almost seems to be a midpoint in Jesus' ministry, halfway between his baptism and his resurrection, two other occasions when God intervenes directly in mysterious and hard-to-explain ways. Just after this, Luke writes that "he set his face to go to Jerusalem" (9:51). After this point, all that Luke tells us is a prelude to Jesus' final entry into the city of his crucifixion and resurrection.

Luke tries to describe the disciples' account of what had happened on the mountain. Only Peter, James, and John were present with Jesus, so Luke must have relied on hearing one of their eyewitness accounts. He uses words reminiscent of the Old Testament descriptions of seeing God's glory: "dazzling white," "cloud," and "voice." Peter was so befuddled he hardly knew what words to use or what to say.

The story of the Transfiguration comes at a unique moment in Jesus' ministry: as mentioned in the study book, Jesus had just completed a number of miracles and talked about his future death (although the disciples did not understand this future occurrence until it happened). One week after these events, while on a hill praying, Jesus was transfigured, although the Scripture does not use that word to report it. Rather, it says that "the appearance of his face changed, and his clothes became dazzling white" (9:29). This recalls the experience of Moses on Mount Sinai, who was still so radiant when he returned from the mountain that the Israelites could not look at him (Exodus 34:29-35).

The presence of Moses and Elijah conferring with Jesus evokes the great traditions of the Hebrew people: the Law, received from God by Moses, and the prophetic witness exemplified in Elijah. Jesus' recent miracles of feeding the multitudes and calming the sea also call to mind events of the Exodus escape and reception of manna in the wilderness as well as Elijah's feeding and healing persons during a time of grave famine (1 Kings 17).

The other elements—the clouds, the voice, the command to "listen to him"—all tied together the past and future of Israel. God has spoken to the Prophets to lead Israel to a new depth of relationship and expectation with God. After these notable guests depart the mountain, Jesus apparently is ready to supersede both the Law and the Prophets. Could it be that the Transfiguration experience was to strengthen Jesus in a unique way in order to complete his work on earth?

Beginning the Lesson

▶ Ask group members to read Luke 9:28-36. Ask if they have any immediate questions. What are their first reactions to the Scripture itself?

Developing the Lesson

▶ Tell the group that the purpose of this session is to spend some time simply studying this mysterious side of God as found in the story of the Transfiguration.

Words for Bible Times

▶ Invite someone to retell in his or her own words the story of the Transfiguration. Ask the rest of the participants to refine the story, add details, make corrections. Have on hand a Bible dictionary and a commentary to add depth to your understanding of this event, and add information from the "Bible Background." Then discuss these questions:

What does the word *transfiguration* **mean?** Explain that the word itself is a later theological term to apply to this one story.

What is the significance of the presence of Elijah and Moses?

What are the key images and words of this story? What other images and events do they evoke?

How did the persons involved in this event act and react? What might you have done if you witnessed such a thing?

What does the story of Jesus' transfiguration teach us about God? about Jesus? about us?

Why do you think Jesus was "transfigured"?

How comfortable are you with having things in the Bible that are not easily explainable in plain language and experiences?

Words for Our Time

▶ Ask someone to read out loud this section from the study book. Consider the Transfiguration as a prophetic and preparatory event for the disciples ("Listen to him") to understand better the nature of Jesus as the Christ and of what he was about to do for the whole people of God. God used this profound experience to strengthen the disciples for their ministry, which was just now in its infant stages. Then discuss these questions:

How does God strengthen us in our lives today?

Does God use mysterious, miraculous ways for us? If so, give an example.

What should the church do with this story in terms of worship, teaching, and outreach?

What are some of the "mysterious" things that we do in our own congregation that are not easily explained, and yet are part of building up of the community of faith? (Possible answers include: Holy Communion, baptism, prayer, laying on of hands, ordination, and others)

How does God's mystery intersect the "ordinary" things we do as a community of faith? in other places of life? (Possible answers include the profound experiences that are evoked in music or prayer; national or political events that bring about liberation)

If this story were not in the New Testament, what would the church, and our present twentieth-century faith lose? or gain?

Words for My Life

▶ Form small groups of three or four persons. Invite them to talk with each other about the time when they felt the closest to God. Ask them to explain both why they felt close at that time and what that closeness did for their faith life. After they have spent enough time discussing that topic, ask them to go back in their minds to that close time with God and to think about whether there were any difficult experiences or challenges in their lives that occurred shortly afterward. Not everyone will have a

challenge to report, but it would be interesting to hear of episodes of closeness in which they were strengthened for what was to come. While they are still in small groups, ask:

Where do you see God most clearly?

Where and who in the past has most clearly shown Jesus Christ to you?

Have you ever experienced a time when you were able to bring God's love and power into other persons' lives, even if you did not know about it at the time? Tell the group that the answer to that question is not meant to encourage boasting or gloating, but rather should be seen as a time when God was simply able to use us as God used a cloud and dazzling light to strengthen Jesus and the disciples on Mount Tabor.

Concluding the Lesson

▶ Invite the group members to continue to think this coming week of times in which God has been revealed to them in ordinary or mysterious ways. They may also wish to spend time thinking about how God may use them to be revealed in someone else's life.

Prayer

▶ Pray together: "Gracious God, grant us the insight and the peace of mind and heart to experience your love, both seen and unseen, and so be strengthened for the task of ministry ahead of us. Amen."

How Much Faith Is Enough?

Luke 17:5-6

Purpose of the Lesson

The purpose of this lesson is to invite adults to consider their own faith as a powerful tool in doing the will of God in our world today.

Bible Background

The disciples very appropriately ask Jesus to increase their faith. When we talk about faith, we usually mean one (or perhaps both) of two things. Faith is often used synonymously with belief; that is, faith is the knowledge and assent to a particular way of thinking or a specific truth. Faith can also refer to the trust born of and cultivated in a relationship, especially a relationship with God. An added dimension to faith as trust has to do with righteousness. A prominent example in the Old Testament that is referred to many times in the New Testament is the faith of Abraham. So great was Abraham's faith that God "reckoned it to him as righteousness" (Genesis 15:6).

Throughout the Old Testament and into the New Testament readings, faith is the core virtue of those who were led by God throughout the history of Israel. Either they had great faith, such as Joseph, Joshua, Deborah, and Anna, or they tried to grow in their faith, as did Moses and the Samaritan woman at the well. Those who are seen as the villains of the Bible, like Ahab and Pharaoh, are the ones who had an opportunity to believe, but who forfeited or denied a relationship with God.

Much of the early writings of Paul affirm that faith (trust in God) is a gift of grace initiated by God (particularly in Romans), which we could never manufacture ourselves. By faith we are called to trust and to base our future actions on the assurance that God is in relationship with us, is for us, and will do certain dependable things, such as forgiving us of sin, supporting us in our life's struggles, and calling us to tasks that have meaning and purpose.

Although it is true that we can and should strengthen faith, the very presence of faith, or trust in someone else, occurs because of the relationship we have with God. The author of Hebrews writes that faith is "the assurance of things hoped for, the conviction of things not seen" (Hebrews 11:1). In this definition, faith becomes the key resource for our relationship with God in the first place, and not merely an outcome of it.

In whichever way we intend to use faith, whether as the source or as the expression of our relationship with God, it remains an integral part of that God-human bond.

Beginning the Lesson

▶ Tell the group members that this session is an opportunity for us to talk about our faith as we look at the faith of the followers of Christ. Invite them to keep their ears and minds open for ways in which they believe their faith could be strengthened and used more effectively.

Developing the Lesson

▶ Invite the participants to try to quantify "faith" using their own size categories. For example, how much would a mustard seed-sized faith accomplish? a wheelbarrow full? a train car load? (This really is an impossible task, but it should illuminate the perils of "keeping score" in faith.)

Words for Bible Times

▶ Ask someone to read Luke 17:1-6, in order to expand the Scripture's context for today's verses. Ask participants to try to define the word *faith* as they understand it. Then use the information from the "Bible Background" and this section in the study book. Have a commentary and a Bible dictionary on hand for further information.

▶ Point out that Jesus seems to tell the disciples that though they think they have faith, they really do not have much. If they had just "a mustard seed's-worth" of faith they could uproot a huge tree-sized problem. Then ask the group these questions:

How do you define *faith*?
What seems to be the question of the disciples? Are they asking for faith? to understand the nature of forgiveness?
What is the relationship

between the forgiveness verses and the faith verses?

Did the disciples really ask the right question, do you think? What would have been a more valid and important question if they did not ask the right one?

How do you expect the disciples thought Jesus would increase their faith?

What is Jesus' response?

Does Jesus sidestep the issue of faith, or does he simply lead them to a different understanding of faith itself? If the group is not familiar with the reference to the mustard seed as a symbol of faith, read out loud the portion in this section of the study book that deals with the mustard seed.

Was the faith of the disciples enough to do what Jesus was asking them to do? If so, in what way was it sufficient?

Would the faith of the disciples really be able to throw a mulberry tree into the sea? What does this mean to you?

Words for Our Time

► Ask group members to use words or phrases that would adequately describe or define a "person of faith." Push them to go beyond the simple descriptions of "kind, gentle, forgiving," and so on, to what they would do and how they would act in the world. Encourage them to put an image or a person in their mind that they see to have a truly "big" faith and to describe their activities as well as their qualities. Use the chalkboard or a large sheet of paper to record their responses. When they finish their descriptions, ask:

What does a mustard seed have to do with these descriptions?

What is it about that mustard seed that is inviting and transforming to persons of faith? (Possible answer: people of faith just do not believe something— they act it out!)

If you were to interview someone with tremendous faith, how do you expect they would respond to your assertion that they were very faithful? Might they quickly agree or demure?

Discuss whether this statement is true: "Christ needs our availability more than our ability." Which of those two words represents faith better for you?

How much faith do we need to have in order to be "faithful" people? Is it more than what we have now?

Words for My Life

► Form small groups of two or three, and have participants discuss these questions:

Do you believe you are presently doing what God has called you to do in your life? If so, is there still more that God wants you to do? What would that be? If not, what is keeping you from responding to God's call?

When have you had the most trouble holding on to your faith? What were the circum-

stances when it just felt as though your faith was being stretched and even broken?

How do we discover what God wants us to do in the first place?

What role does discernment have in our spiritual lives?

Do you believe most people lack faith, or lack the inclination to use the faith that God has already given them? Explain.

► Bring small groups together and ask them to respond to the final statement in the study book: "let our prayer move away from 'Increase our faith,' to 'Open our eyes so that we may see Christ wherever we are.' "

Concluding the Lesson

► Invite group members to ask themselves this question each morning over the next week: "What does God want me to do this day?"

Tell them that by focusing their attention on seeking God's intentions for them, they will be able to focus their faith in the same way Jesus spoke of faith and the mulberry tree.

Prayer

► Close with this prayer: "Our Loving Christ, use our mustard-seed faith and our hesitant yet willing hearts to serve you in truth as your disciples today. We pray with confidence and faith before you. Amen."

Where Is the Kingdom of God?

Luke 17:20-21

Purpose of the Lesson

The purpose of this lesson is to help adults understand Jesus' pronouncement of the kingdom of God and its place in our lives today.

Bible Background

Probably no phrase was spoken more often by Jesus than the words "kingdom of God." Jesus frequently preached the coming of the Kingdom, the ways in which the Kingdom might be known to us, how the Kingdom grows and develops. By his presence in the world, the Kingdom has come; with that coming, the normal way of the world's operation must change. God is bringing back the relationship between God and humankind, and the way of living that all humans long for, but are unable to live out, due to their tendency to sin.

What is the kingdom of God? The word for *kingdom* in the Scriptures is the Greek *basileia*, which means not so much a physical territory (as the kingdom of Great Britain) as it does a "reign," or a "rule by a king." It is a way of life, a way of existence for the people of that kingdom.

The terms *kingdom of God* and *kingdom of heaven* are synonyms—two ways of saying the same thing. We often use a verbal shortcut when we talk about "going to heaven," or about God being in heaven. By that, we mean "the kingdom of heaven."

Seldom does the Bible use the term *heaven* to describe the realm of God. Usually *heaven*, or *heavens*, designates the sky, although there is a more transcendent meaning. Where God is, there is the kingdom of God or the kingdom of heaven—the place where God "dwells" (which is not the sky).

The kingdom of heaven reflects the transformational presence of God in this world. But hasn't God always ruled the earth? Why now has the kingdom of God come in Jesus?

The Gospel writers share the focus that Jesus' central message is about the kingdom of God and that this is an eschatological message—concerned with the End Times. With Christ's coming, God has intended and enabled a new way of life. It will be a rule or a reign in which all of the earth, instead of turning away, will turn to God, recognize God's place in their lives, and so live at peace—shalom—with one another.

It is in the coming of Jesus that the new kingdom of God is proclaimed and announced. The Son of God will bring that to pass through his teachings, his healings, his miracles, his sacrificial life. Jesus' role in the advent of the Kingdom is different from John the Baptist's. John preached that persons should get ready for the coming Kingdom. Jesus proclaims that the Kingdom is here—a present and an eschatological reality—and it demands our attention and response.

Where the kingdom of God is, God's will is done. The words of the Lord's Prayer become a couplet: "Thy kingdom come, thy will be done on earth as it is in heaven." Each phrase means almost the same thing, for in God's kingdom, all will know God's will.

Beginning the Lesson

▶ Ask group members to define *kingdom*; write their answers on the chalkboard or on poster paper. Some may talk about a physical boundary, or a span of time, or an actual rule or reign. Say that today you will be looking at a specific kingdom, known as the kingdom of God. Then open the session with a short prayer.

Developing the Lesson

▶ Clarify the terms *kingdom of God, kingdom of heaven*, and *heaven* so that all participants are using a similar vocabulary. (Use the information in "Bible Background.")

Words for Bible Times

▶ Ask a volunteer to read aloud Luke 17:20-21. Ask for any initial reactions to the Scripture: Have you heard this passage? Do you understand it completely? Next, ask group members to review this section in the study book. Call their attention to the role of the Messiah in the kingdom of God. Use the "Bible Background" and a Bible commentary for more complete information. Then ask participants to discuss these questions:

What appears to be the Pharisees' understanding of the kingdom of God?

What was the Pharisees' point of attack with Jesus concerning the Kingdom?

What do you think they hoped to prove by his explanation? What happened instead?

Do you think Jesus' explanation of the kingdom of God was acceptable to those who were listening? Explain.

Do you think his unwillingness to allow the Kingdom to be identified as a political entity would have dissuaded some folks from following? Explain.

Do you think most folks understood Jesus' preaching that the kingdom of God was already in place and growing? Why or why not?

Why do you think God acts in ways that sometimes confound human expectations and plans?

Words for Our Time

▶ Use the "Bible Background" and the information in this section of the study book to explain a bit more fully the concept of the kingdom of God, its place, and its power. Discuss the class members' understanding of how the kingdom of God exists in our world today. At least touch on these themes:

● God reclaiming the world
● The Kingdom and salvation
● Radical reordering of life

▶ Then ask these questions to follow up the discussion:

How is the Kingdom here now and also a future expectation?

What would a "kingdom life" be like for you?

What evidence do you see that the Kingdom is here?

Words for My Life

▶ Form small groups and ask group members to talk about a time when they were keenly aware of God's presence and work in their lives, such as in something creative, in a generous or loving act, or in a moment of forgiveness. Then ask them to discuss a time when they believed they missed seeing God's will and grace because they were distracted or busy with some other part of their living. Bring the group back together and ask:

What, do you think, enabled you to see God's activity clearly? What inhibited it?

Who has helped you at significant times to see the presence of God and the kingdom of God?

In what ways can you announce the Kingdom to others?

Concluding the Lesson

▶ Invite group members to read through Matthew, Mark, or Luke this coming week to study the statements Jesus makes about the kingdom of God and to open themselves to share that Kingdom's presence more fully.

Prayer

▶ Pray the Lord's Prayer as you close this session, and ask the group members to listen for the part of the prayer concerning God's kingdom.

How Much Should I Give to the Church?

Luke 21:1-4

Purpose of the Lesson

The purpose of this lesson is to help adults consider their own rationale for offering their gifts and tithes within the Christian community.

Bible Background

We catch a good glimpse of Jesus by paying close attention to what caught his attention, and money was a frequent theme. *Money* was not a bad word for Jesus. In fact, a significant number of Jesus' parables and word images contain references to salary, investments, debt, and treasure. Jesus knew and acknowledged that "where your treasure is, there your heart will be also" (Matthew 6:21). Money has been part of the life of almost every person since money was invented. We all know that from ages past, money is what makes the world go around.

Operating the Temple in Jerusalem cost a great deal of money. Herod the Great, who was a tremendous builder (building Masada and the aqueduct at Caesarea), had rebuilt the Temple. Herod's Temple rivaled or surpassed the Temple built during the time of Solomon. It was a grand complex, with a huge plaza built after Herod had expanded the acreage of Mount Moriah where the Temple was situated. He built new walls to support the Temple Mount and filled in and leveled off the plaza area. It was tremendous; and

even today, the sheer size of the Temple Mount is fantastic to see.

The Temple complex, so vast and opulent, must have had both a large support staff and a large maintenance budget for it to remain such a wonder. Who would pay to run the Temple? The expectation was that the people of Israel would fund the Temple through their gifts. The widow in today's story was simply doing what she had been asked to do.

The woman's offering was not given to purchase sacrificial offerings for the altar, since she used a coin that was not allowed in the purchase of those animals. The only coin that was accepted by the Temple was the Tyrian half-shekel, a coin of high grade silver, which necessitated the business of the money changers outside the walls of the Temple. Foreign travelers to the Temple had to have the right currency.

The widow, Jesus said, gave the right gift—two leptons, each worth less than half a cent. These copper coins were the smallest denomination of coins in circulation, yet they were regarded by Jesus as the greatest gift.

This was not to say that the gifts of the others were insignificant. The Scripture does not indicate that the others' contributions were small or were given grudgingly. But, Jesus said, the others gave out of their abundance, that is, from what was left over after all their needs and most of their wants were satisfied. The amount might have been great, but God was the last recipient on their lists.

Beginning the Lesson

▶ Ask participants if they can recall the very first time they placed something in the offering plate at church (hopefully it was earlier than last week!). Ask them if they can remember what it felt like, or if the reason for giving had been explained to them at all before the offering plate was passed.

Developing the Lesson

▶ Tell the participants that this session deals with something near and dear to everyone's heart: money. It will spur them to consider what they give as offerings, but not in the way they think.

Words for Bible Times

▶ Have group members read Luke 21:1-4. Using the "Bible Background" and information from this section of the study book, explain the rationale and background for giving the gifts in the Temple in the first place. Also explain the place of a widow at the time of Jesus. Then ask:

Was there anything wrong with the gifts the other people gave at the Temple that day? If not, why do we sometimes feel that the rich did not do their part?

Why did Jesus commend the widow and hold up her gift as significant?

What is it about the widow's

gift that is significant for our understanding of the story? (Possible answer: it went beyond a contribution to the church to become an offering and an act of worship to God.)

Were the others who gave their gifts any less blessed than she was? Define *stewardship*: *Stewardship* is the practice of simply returning to God for God's use all that belongs to God in the first place.

Should the widow have given both (or either) of the coins? If she had nothing else, do you think God would have required it of her? What would she live on?

Did the woman practice good stewardship that day? Would that have been something that you could do? Why or why not?

In what way was the widow blessed by her gift that day?

Words for Our Time

▶ Ask someone in the group to read aloud the first two paragraphs in this section of the study book, ending with "pledge or give outright to the church." Discuss whether giving money or contributions to the church is unbiblical. Please help group members understand that the purpose of the statement is not to dissuade them from making gifts to God. Ask:

What is the difference, to you, between giving to the church and giving to God?

Is there a difference, in your opinion, or is it just a matter of semantics?

▶ Invite group members to think and talk about the way in which they give to support the ministry of the church, including the frequency (weekly, monthly) and form (cash, check, time). Ask:

How do you define *abundance*? **How do you determine priorities in when and where to give?**

What would you say is the difference between abundant giving and sacrificial giving? What does the Bible ask for?

Which ways of giving are most helpful in making the gift feel as real and significant as it is?

What, do you think, motivates people to give money offerings to God?

When persons do not contribute money, even to a church in which they worship and receive services, what effect does that have on the church? What effect do you imagine it has on God?

Do you think those same folks give to God in a different way?

If a poor, homeless person or someone with a subsistence income stopped by your church to worship and to ask for help, do you think God would expect them to put in the offering whatever money they had in their pockets? Explain.

Words for My Life

▶ Form groups of two or three. Ask group members to discuss their views of stewardship. Have them discuss these questions as well and then to compare responses with the other small group members.

If you were not allowed to give money as a means of offering to the church, what would you be able to give instead? Suggest that these other "offerings," no less important or valuable than their financial gifts, are needed by the church in order for the church to fulfill its responsibility of ministry of Christ in the world. Mention the four categories of "prayer, presence, gifts, and service" as stewardship opportunities.

Concluding the Lesson

▶ Invite the participants to recall during the week the gifts of God with which they have been entrusted and how they might be used to support God through the church.

Prayer

▶ Pray together: "Make us generous, O God, not simply with the gifts we have to offer, but with the blessed love you have first given us; in Christ's name. Amen."

16

Are Christians Really Supposed to Share All Their Possessions?

Acts 4:32-37

Purpose of the Lesson

The purpose of this lesson is to give adults an opportunity to think about how they share with each other the gifts that God has first given to us.

Bible Background

It was a natural expression and outgrowth of their faith experience that led the early Christians to move into a communal type of economic system for a time. Most of the disciples came from the same area; some were related to each other. The early Christians, many of whom were Jews, "devoted themselves to the apostles' teaching and fellowship, to the breaking of bread, and the prayers" (Acts 2:42), thus continuing a form of their familiar rituals. Other rituals included several accepted means of atonement in Judaism, such as almsgiving. In addition to prayer and fasting, righteous deeds, either personal or social, could serve as expiatory or atoning acts. One could atone for violations of Torah law by doing deeds of kindness to others in need.

While the Jewish Christians were given a new law through Jesus Christ, the Torah, with all of its personal, communal, and moral codes, would have been the bedrock of their behavior. (See for example, Leviticus 25:35-38.) They were other-oriented and accustomed to giving.

In addition, the disciples and the others who had been following Jesus for the past three years had become a close spiritual family under the leadership of their Master. In his death, they were devastated together, and in his Resurrection and post-Resurrection appearances, they were strengthened together. Then, after Pentecost had come, and the Holy Spirit had been gifted to them, there was even a closer bond and sense of anticipation of the imminent return of their Lord. To pool their resources would have been a natural thing. They loved one another.

On the other hand, most likely very few of those who were part of the early church had anything of exceptional value to begin with! Remember that they had been disciples of an itinerant preacher for three years. They had enough to live on (although once they had to go into a field in order to find grain to eat), but certainly they were not looking to find ways to invest their funds! This becomes a bit more evident when Barnabas was singled out for a personal mention by Luke for selling a field and giving the money to the apostles. Pointing out the generosity of this gift from Barnabas (and the selfish gesture by Ananias and Sapphira) imply that pooling resources of this magnitude may not have been a typical occurrence, but in fact, was something of significant note, as in our

receiving an unusually large bequest given to the church.

Nonetheless, the story offers the reader a flavor of the exciting and almost euphoric time of the very early church and the members who gave their lives for it. As alluded to earlier, the story that follows our Scripture for today is an equally fascinating glimpse into fundraising and finances in the early church, although not quite with the same openness and love. Ananias and Sapphira sold their property but held back a portion from the communal gift. Their duplicity was their undoing, reminiscent of Achan's experience in Joshua 7.

Beginning the Lesson

► Ask the group members each to take a piece of paper and to write as many items as they can in two minutes that their particular family owns communally. They may include anything that is considered to be owned or shared jointly by two or more people in their home or family. After two minutes, ask them to stop and to save their list to look at a bit later in today's session.

Developing the Lesson

► Tell the group members that today's session deals with a Christian concept that the Christian church rarely uses today: sharing possessions with other believers.

Words for Bible Times

▶ Begin this section by setting the context for the Scripture lesson: The setting for the Scripture is Jerusalem, a short time after the event of Pentecost in which the disciples received the gift of the Holy Spirit and the inspiration to boldly preach the gospel. The church is founded, and many miracles and signs of God's presence are being seen. Ask someone in the group to read Acts 4:32-37. Then give a review of the "Bible Background" above and of this section in the study book. Then ask:

Does this description sound exciting to you, or worrisome? Why?

Does it sound like something that churches today should think about doing?

What do you think was the motivation for this type of economic arrangement among the early Christians?

▶ The early Christians were characterized as being "of one heart and soul," which seems the clear indicator of why they were able to share. Have group members describe this kind of unity more completely and identify any ways in which the church today shares that characterization. Then invite the group to look closely at the Scripture lesson and to list on a chalkboard or large piece of paper the positive qualities and blessings that the community took on through this time. Afterward, discuss these questions:

Did those blessings happen because the believers began to act communally, or did they begin to act communally because those blessings had occurred? What is the reason behind your answer?

Words for Our Time

▶ Invite a member of the group to read the letter from the pastor in this section of the study book. After the laughter subsides, ask for their reaction to such a letter being sent out to the members of the church. Ask:

Is this an absurd or a courageous letter? Ask participants to define the word *fair* in terms of such an economic arrangement in the church.

Does *fair* mean that all share equally in the blessings of the whole, or does it mean that the individual work and efforts of members gives them the right to receive those individual blessings? Explain.

Do possessions mean more than they should to us as Christians? Explain.

What possessions should we cherish, and what are simply "ballast" for our lives?

▶ Ask the group members to look again at the list that they developed of household assets. Discuss how much of those things are important for their family's financial strength, how much of it is necessary for their comfort, and how much of it is simply unnecessary.

▶ Say to the group: "The disciples were living in a time in which they believed Christ's return was imminent—perhaps moments or days away. If we truly believed that same thing, do you think it would it be easier for us to share economic and physical resources with others in community or in extended families? How do we honestly make use of the things that have been given into our care by God?

Words for My Life

▶ Ask class members to listen as you read this section from the study book. Ask them to set aside the question of whether we should give away our "stuff" and talk instead with each other about the role of trust within the community of faith.

How much trust do we have for each other that our needs will be met?

Instead of sharing our possessions, are we willing to share our lives and hearts, knowing that as the need arises in our lives, there will be those within our faith community who will come to care for us?

What is the root of this kind of stewardship?

Concluding the Lesson

▶ Ask each member of the group to reconsider her or his gifts to the congregation and trust of the body of Christ. Ask everyone to pray about how we could live our lives more closely in the early church's example of love.

Prayer

▶ Pray this prayer: "Give us what we need to live, Gracious God, and give us hearts willing to give what we have for the needs of others. Amen."

How Can I Be Worthy Enough to Receive Holy Communion?

1 Corinthians 11:17-34

Purpose of the Lesson

The purpose of this lesson is to give adults the opportunity to talk about Holy Communion as a gift of worship of God in Jesus Christ.

Bible Background

Corinth was a great cosmopolitan city in Greece at the time of Paul. The church in that city must have been filled with some awfully unusual characters! Paul spends a great deal of time in his letters trying to "straighten out" the Corinthians in terms of infighting, sexual immorality, lawsuits, and marriage. In 1 Corinthians 11:17-34, Paul addresses their abuses of the Eucharist.

The Eucharist—Holy Communion or the Lord's Supper—was the first and most powerful act of worship that existed for the early Christians. The transformation of the Jewish Passover meal into a special worship moment that recalled the suffering and death of Jesus must have been a riveting moment for the disciples who were in the upper room. They gave the changed ritual to the newly gathered group of the followers of Christ; and today we participate in the same sacrament, practically unchanged in its wording and meaning since the time of Christ.

The description in First Corinthians is for us the earliest mention of the Lord's Supper in the Bible. (The Gospels and the Book of Acts were written later than First Corinthians). The study book explains the problem with the church in Corinth, but it may help to realize that the earliest "communions" occurred whenever the group of followers gathered.

They took literally the commandment "Whenever you eat, whenever you drink," and so Communion became a regular occurrence. The purpose was to celebrate the great gift Jesus Christ had offered to the believers, but Paul strongly implies that their celebration was carried to excess. Rather than being a time of harmony and unity, the meal was observed and eaten in a way that amplified their differences.

This was a congregation that evidently did not share all things in common, for it is obvious that some members were wealthy and some were needy. They met, most likely in a wealthier member's home, and each brought his or her own provisions for the meal. But rather than sharing their resources, those who had a lot of food indulged; those who had little went hungry during the "fellowship meal." After the meal, there was evidently the symbolic meal of the loaf and the cup.

It was in this ritual sharing that the community was particularly to offer thanksgiving (the meaning of Eucharist) for the salvific effects of Jesus' body and blood. In taking the elements of bread and wine, the believers symbolically participated in this dying and rising, which should have emphasized their unity as the one body of Christ. But their abuse of the ritual only emphasized their disunity. Paul's comments were intended to remind the Corinthians that in this sacramental meal, the believers were to demonstrate their Christian commonality in a way that overcame social and economic differences, both between them as individuals and within the congregation.

Beginning the Lesson

▶ Ask the group: When you think of Holy Communion, what words come to your mind? Write their responses on the chalkboard or a large piece of paper, and save these responses for a bit later in the session. Ask them also to take a few minutes to talk about their earliest memories of Communion, or perhaps the first or most special time they shared Holy Communion.

Developing the Lesson

▶ Tell the participants that they will be examining the ways in which they come prepared to receive the gift of Communion, and how that compares with the problems the Corinthians had.

Words for Bible Times

▶ Introduce the Scripture by using some of the information from the "Bible Background" and in the first section of the study book. Be sure to stress the problem in the inequities experienced by some of the early Corinthian believers in those communal meals. Ask someone in the group to read 1 Corinthians 11:17-34 aloud, in order to gain a bit more perspective on Paul's lecture to the church.

▶ Ask the group members to discuss the main problems the Corinthians had and to decide whether they think it was truly a monumental problem that would require Paul's response. Be sure they understand the importance of the fact that Holy Communion was being violated in a certain way over the course of these actions. Then ask these questions:

What, do you think, should have been the heart's intention of the Corinthians as they gathered for the meal?
What actually became the intention?
How does Paul define "worthiness" in the Scripture as it refers to sharing in the Communion meal? (You may wish to refer to this section of the study book if there are problems in answering this question.)
Is that definition of worthiness to take Communion still valid for us today? Explain.

Words for Our Time

▶ Invite someone to read the story from this section of the study book. Ask the group to discuss the story from the point of view of each of the participants. Then discuss these questions as a whole group:

Was Greg justified, do you think, in being upset about the actions of the "Bible study ladies," or do you believe they did have a valid point? Give reasons for your response.
What do you believe it means to be "worthy to receive Communion"?
Do you believe, as the writer does, that participation in Communion has more to do with intent than of knowledge? If not, what do you believe?
How much knowledge about the sacrament of Communion do we need in order to participate in it fully?
Should children, who do not have the knowledge of the specifics of Holy Communion, but who are members of the family of faith, be allowed to share in the meal? Explain.
What about visitors to our congregations, or persons who have not previously been part of the church?
How can we better educate our worshiping congregation about the aspects of this important part of our faith life? Is that necessary? Explain your answers.

Words for My Life

▶ Ask the participants to form small groups of two or three and refer them to this section in the study book. Have them talk in their small groups about their own view and approach to Communion—not what they believe others should do, but how they come to the Communion table. Ask them to consider *worthiness* in terms of coming to worship as though it were an obligation or a chore to be accomplished. Use the following questions to sustain the discussion:

What does God expect from us anytime we worship—whether Communion is celebrated or not?
How would centering on worthiness affect the unity and harmony of your worshiping local body of Christ?

▶ Ask small group members to also look at the answers they wrote about their earliest thoughts of Communion, and ask:

How many of those memories were of "unworthy" times of sharing in Communion?
How many of them do you think God was pleased to eat with us?

Concluding the Lesson

▶ Read again the words of Paul from 1 Corinthians 11:23-25.

Prayer

▶ Pray this prayer: "We thank you for your gifts, Gracious God, and for your love that will not let us go. Keep our hearts open and ready to receive your gifts, including the gift of your holy meal; in Christ's name. Amen."

How Important Is Belief in an Afterlife?

1 Corinthians 15:12-20

Purpose of the Lesson

The purpose of this lesson is to help adults explore Christian beliefs about life after death and to find hope as we live our lives today.

Bible Background

"Afterlife" can take on a wide variety of forms, if we set the Scripture aside. From reincarnation to ghosts to "spirits" and "life essences," there have been many ways in which the human mind has tried to figure out what happens to us after we have completed our life on earth.

The New Testament Scripture appears to be consistent, however, as it talks about an afterlife that is completely linked to the presence of God. Jesus himself talked about "eternal life," and "coming to the Father" by way of Christ. I think a powerful statement that Jesus makes through his references to afterlife is that it happens in relationship with God. This is unique and easily distinguished from the other types of "afterlife" mentioned earlier. If you live in one of those ways, you are on your own. As a Christian, you are never apart from God.

The early church spent an enormous amount of time and discussion over the question of Christ's resurrection and our eternal hope. The Apostles' Creed in part is a means of answering other theories about Jesus' death and life and ours in the way it (and other creeds)

spell out the orthodox tradition of the church.

Corinth was a super-urban city with a tremendous influx of foreign trade and cultural influences. There were literally dozens of "mystery religions" that dealt with all sorts of themes of death and resurrection. It was in this setting that Paul carefully wrote 1 Corinthians 15 for the congregation to study (and to accept!). The themes Paul touches on are the most profound for our faith: the link between sin, death, and resurrection; the power of God in the resurrection of Jesus Christ; the benefits of Christ's resurrection for believers; and the hope inherent in the eschatological (end times) promise that the faithful will be raised.

It is perhaps important to note that the Christian faith for nearly two thousand years has defined its belief and faith over and against the prevailing religious belief systems that arise in the world from time to time. That is the work of theology, or "God study."

Beginning the Lesson

▶ First of all, acknowledge that some group members will have lost to death someone close to them, perhaps recently. Let these persons know that you hope this session will be a comfort and a strength to them and that you would appreciate learning their special, particular thoughts surrounding death, life, and "afterlife."

▶ Ask participants to form groups of four or five and to talk for a while about their views and attitudes, not toward death itself, but specifically what they believe happens to us after we die.

Developing the Lesson

▶ Tell group members that we will study the belief and writing of Paul as he talks about the importance of Christ's resurrection for our lives.

Words for Bible Times

▶ Read, or invite someone to read aloud 1 Corinthians 15:12-20. Review the information in "Bible Background" and in the study book. Have a commentary on hand to answer other questions about this complex passage. Ask participants to listen carefully to what appears to be the argument or problem in Corinth that Paul is trying to answer. (The purpose of a number of his letters to the churches was not so much to teach as to correct and encourage. A possible answer to what the problem was: a segment of the church refused to believe that the dead would be raised to life.)

▶ Lead a discussion of what participants believe it was like in Corinth at this time with this problem. Ask:

What is the nature of the discussion? How big of a problem do you think it was?
How might it have affected

the worship? the cohesiveness of the community?

What impact would it have on the development of the Christian faith itself?

How seriously does Paul take the problem?

Do you understand the intricacies of Paul's argument? Do you think it persuasive?

Is Paul's point valid (especially in verses 14 and 17) where he holds up Christ's resurrection as a key to faith and forgiveness itself? Explain.

How different would our faith in God be if indeed, Christ had not been raised from the dead?

Is the resurrection of Jesus Christ an issue of our future hope, or of our present relationship with God, or both? Explain.

Words for Our Time

▶ Ask the group members to read this section of the study book if they have not yet done so. Discuss the importance of Christ's resurrection and the promise of eternal life for our faith community today. Then ask:

How does Christ's resurrection affect your understanding of God's power and love for us today?

Is your understanding of salvation tied to the belief in Christ's resurrection? Explain your answer.

How does a belief in God's ability and willingness to offer us an "afterlife" answer our normal human emotions and thoughts about fear, loneliness,

meaning, separation, and loss?

Does our church community do a good job of "getting the word out" about resurrection, or do we keep it a fairly closely regarded secret?

What is the purpose of the church as it deals with the truth and faith surrounding "afterlife"?

Words for My Life

▶ Distribute pieces of paper and pencils, and ask each person to take five minutes or so to write a paragraph describing their faith concerning what happens after we die. It does not have to be in a polished form, but ask them to take seriously the whole issue of life after death—God's role, Christ's role, and the benefits and responsibilities we have as the followers of Christ. Let them know that they will be asked to share their beliefs with one or two other persons in a few minutes.

▶ After they have completed that assignment, form groups of two or three and ask small group members to discuss what they have written. Be sensitive to those for whom this assignment may be difficult, either because they have experienced death recently, or because they just simply do not have an idea about resurrection and life after death. Be sure to let the group know that we are all at different places on our faith journey, and some of us just simply may not have had the time and opportunity to form a systematic, well-framed theology of death

and eternal life. What you are simply asking them to do is to share with each other what they believe to be true up until now, knowing that growth can and should always happen. Ask them:

Look carefully at the similarities and the differences among each other's statements. How have you each come to believe those statements to be true?

▶ While participants are still in the small groups, either read aloud or invite them to read silently the account of the death of the writer's father in this section of the study book. Then discuss:

What affirmations are found in this story?

Think about your life, your experiences of death, and the writing of Paul in Corinthians. What can you affirm about God's love and God's power concerning death and life?

Concluding the Lesson

▶ Invite the group members to keep their writings and to look back over them during the course of this next week. Ask them to continue to think about ways in which they can use affirmations of faith in God to help in their everyday lives.

Prayer

▶ Pray the Lord's Prayer as you close this session.

What Is the Resurrection of the Body?

1 Corinthians 15:35-57

Purpose of the Lesson

The purpose of this lesson is to help adults explore the biblical idea of the "resurrected body" and what it means for our future hope.

Bible Background

Paul completes his discussion with the church at Corinth with perhaps the most mysterious concepts outside of the books of Revelation and Daniel: the resurrection of the body. The literal belief in resurrection for individuals as an act of God came into focus during the Intertestamental period, from about the second century before Christ to the days of the early church. The persecution of the Jews in the early part of that time was so brutal (see 2 Maccabees 7 for an example) that they came to believe that if their suffering could not be vindicated by God in this life, then surely it would be so after death. Over the succeeding centuries, belief in resurrection was refined and debated. It was one of the points of contention between the Pharisees and the Sadducees.

As Paul wrote to the Corinthians, he helped create a core theology for the new church to consider and reevaluate over the course of the next nineteen centuries. Paul brought before the church at Corinth a major faith issue, not only about who Jesus is and how God operates, but also about who we are. There were major divisions in the early Christian church that arose over the concepts of what makes a human being. Are we completely physical? Are we divided into physical and spiritual parts that really do not have a lot to do with each other, and the spiritual just inhabits and uses the physical body until it is no longer of any value? Is our physical body bad, and our spiritual body good?

Paul was not just explaining a new concept to new Christians. He was defending the Christian faith in the midst of competing claims about the nature of Christ. The gnostics in particular and Greek thought in general held a dichotomous (two-part) view of the spirit and the body, believing things of the spirit to be good and pure and things of the body to be corrupt and evil. Jewish and Christian thought did not separate the body from the spirit; persons were a unified whole, created in the image of God to be good.

At the same time, the church continued to debate and wrestle with the issue of our eternal hope, that is, What can we expect to happen to us as faithful followers of Jesus Christ after we die? What will happen to the faithful who died before Jesus came? Of course, the most intriguing thing about all of these debates is that, in the final analysis, there is no way to know conclusively and scientifically unless we were to die.

So, how do we come to believe something to be true? One segment of the Christian church believes that we have resources for coming to understand our faith: Scripture, the tradition of the church and faith over the centuries, our own holy and special experiences of God, and the use of reason. Consider all of these resources in cooperation with each other as you study 1 Corinthians 15.

Beginning the Lesson

▶ Ask the group to quickly come up with words or phrases that they think of when they hear the words *resurrection* and *resurrection of the body*. Write those words and phrases on the chalkboard or poster paper.

Developing the Lesson

▶ Tell the participants that the topic of today's session is the resurrection of the body, and that they should keep their list of words and phrases in mind during the session.

Words for Bible Times

▶ Invite a member of the class to read 1 Corinthians 15:35-57 aloud as the others follow along in their own Bibles. Ask for their first responses to the Scripture. Have they ever read or studied this before? Some persons will know the words of the Apostles' Creed, but may have relied on nonscriptural traditions both within and outside the church community to form their views on resurrection and the resurrected body.

▶ Ask group members to define the differences between *resurrection* and *resuscitation*. (Possible definitions may be: resuscitation means bringing back to life someone who has been clinically dead, through medical or other miraculous means. It is a restarting, or reestablishing of a physical living. Resurrection, in Paul's words and in the description of Jesus' resurrection, really means a new creation of sorts, in which someone is still recognized, but has received a new, unique physical/spiritual body as he or she abides with God.) Ask them to determine which one Paul is talking about.

▶ Have at least one commentary on hand to delve deeper into these complex ideas. Review the "Bible Background" here and in this section of the study book. Continue your exploration by asking:

How would you define *perishable* and *imperishable*?
How do you understand Paul's imagery about being "sown" and "raised"?
Are Paul's writings and beliefs different at all from your understanding of the timing of the resurrection of the dead?
Did Paul mean to say that all persons who die will "sleep" until the last trumpet sounds, and then the dead will rise in new bodies? What does this mean?
Do you think Paul's belief is tied at all to the understanding of the early Christians that Christ's return to the earth was imminent? Explain your answer.
Which do you believe to be

true of resurrection: a resting of all souls until that one time, or the general resurrection of the dead into the presence of God at the time of death? Explain.
(Again, be sensitive to those who may have experienced the death of someone close to them recently.)

Words for Our Time

▶ Form small groups of four or five, and ask them to read this section of the study book silently. When all have completed their reading, ask them to talk about what they believe about eternal life and the resurrected body for their own lives. Have them consider these questions:

Is a resurrected body a reward for faith in Jesus Christ?
What would be the use of a resurrected body? What might it be like?
Why would God give it to us? (The study book may give some starting points to answer the above questions.)
Would people approach the whole experience of death and burial differently, do you think, if they had a better understanding of the resurrected body? If so, in what ways would it be different?
When the Apostles' Creed states that we believe in the "resurrection of the body," does it seem clearer to you now? In what ways?

Words for My Life

▶ While participants are still in small groups, ask them to think about what the gift of a resurrected body means for our faith, and our understanding of God's love,

power and future plans for us. Ask:

What would be missing if we were not to be resurrected, and only resuscitated?
How, do you think, do persons who are agnostic or atheistic deal with death and what happens to their loved ones at death? What might be the survivor's source of hope?

▶ The writer of this section of the study book talks about "hope" as one of the first blessings that is received in an acceptance of the resurrected body as part of our faith. Discuss these questions:

In what ways would you see hope as a benefit, and a tool for our lives today? for the future? for the grand sweep of your life?

Concluding the Lesson

▶ Read Paul's words in 1 Corinthians 15:58 as a way of showing Paul's understanding of how we should use the promise of a resurrected body in our lives of faith.

Prayer

▶ Pray this prayer: "O God, your gifts to us are more mysterious than we can imagine. Simply give us the strength and the faith today to know that our future is well cared for, even the future that exists after our death; in Jesus' name. Amen."

Should I Expect Ecstatic Experiences?

2 Corinthians 12:1-10

Purpose of the Lesson

The purpose of this lesson is to explain to adults what Paul means about "ecstatic experiences" and to help adults talk about them in terms of our life and faith.

Bible Background

The Bible is full of the accounts of persons who have had visions and other spiritual revelations and experiences. From Noah to Abraham to Jacob to Saul, Samuel, David, Solomon, Mary, Joseph, Zechariah, Jesus, and a host of other men and women in the Scripture, we can find references to unique and sometimes puzzling ways in which God has intended to work out the purpose of grace and salvation in the world.

You may wish to read some of these accounts in preparation for this session. Here is a list of some of the Scriptures you may wish to review. Not of all these may be classified as specifically "ecstatic experiences" in line with Paul's recounting, but they are significant enough to realize that Paul's experiences were not unusual or one-of-a-kind.

- Genesis 6:11-22
- Genesis 12:1-3; 15:1-21
- Genesis 28:10-17
- Exodus 3:1-12
- 1 Samuel 3:1-18
- 1 Samuel 10:9-16 (make sure that you read this one!)
- Luke 1
- Luke 24:13-32

It is interesting that as Luke details the accounts of Paul's life in the Book of the Acts, these "out of body" experiences are not included. The physical dangers were mentioned; throughout Acts we learn about his beatings, shipwrecks, imprisonments, and narrow escapes. There are those who think that Paul (and others in the Bible) may have had a life-death-life experience. They suggest that he died from one of the attacks and while dead was shown the glories of heaven. But rather than attaining to the life after death, he was required to return to life and complete his work. Such a suggestion is not scholarly, but it has a certain appeal in explaining what otherwise might be unexplainable. Whatever happened, Paul used the experience to make his point about his own spiritual office among the Corinthians.

However strange it may sound to us, the concept of heavenly journeys would have been known and used by Paul's opponents, the false teachers he warned the Corinthians to avoid. Such visions or journeys were popular means of claiming divine authority. But those experiences, which Paul fails to describe in any detail, are not the point, he says. Paul is apparently caricaturing the private ecstatic experience of false teachers as having little to do with the real work of spreading the gospel. Paul's real authority, and that of a true apostle and believer, rests in his boasting of the power of weakness made strong by God's grace.

Unfortunately, a great deal of what Paul says on this subject as a way of presenting his spiritual preeminence is lost on us today, for most of us in orthodox Christianity have no tradition or experience of either the ecstatic experience or of boasting of our weaknesses. We must not, however, discount revelation and the personal insight provided by the Holy Spirit, which Paul says speaks deep in our hearts (Romans 8:26-27). There are and have been deeply spiritual mystics of the Christian faith throughout the centuries who have written of experiences close to these. It is appropriate to remember that there will always remain within our faith the element of mystery.

Beginning the Lesson

▶ Ask the group to define the word *experiences* as a noun. Then ask them to divide into groups of two to talk for a few minutes about one personal, significant spiritual experience that may have been hard to explain. Suggest that persons who have not had such an experience could try to explain what they have heard and understood of someone else's significant spiritual encounter.

Developing the Lesson

▶ Tell the group that the phrase for the day is *ecstatic experiences* and that they will examine at least one experience (Paul's) in regard to the advancement of the Christian faith.

Words for Bible Times

▶ Read aloud 2 Corinthians 12:1-10. Ask participants to identify any phrases in the Scripture that they are in doubt about. Write them on the chalkboard or on a large piece of paper. Use a Bible dictionary and a commentary on Second Corinthians to research and explain those terms.

▶ Ask participants to review this section of the study book. Mention points of interest in the "Bible Background," above. Then discuss these questions:

What does Paul seem to mean about boasting and weakness? What portions of it can you relate to?

What, do you think, is Paul's purpose in writing of these experiences to the Corinthians? Do you agree with him?

How would you describe the nature of the ecstatic experience mentioned by Paul?

What are the ways in which God speaks to us? Are any of them better than any other? Explain.

Words for Our Time

▶ Review this section of the study book. Keep in mind that some persons may very well have had some experiences that they cannot or have not taken time to understand. They may not wish to talk about these experiences with the others, and of course, have that right. Then ask the participants:

What do you understand as the benefit of Paul's special experiences for him?

Have you ever had a vision, revelation, or spiritual insight than warned or advised you of something to come? What was it like? What did you do?

Do all Christians need to experience some sort of "special" revelation in order to have a full and mature faith? Explain.

Some persons choose to live a life of contemplation; others seem to be given the gift of mystical encounter with God. This is part of the "divine economy" within the universal church. How do you understand your part in this divine economy?

If you cannot understand or explain Paul's experiences clearly (or your own) does that somehow discount the experience? Explain.

Words for My Life

▶ Ask the participants to form groups of three and to discuss at least two or three of these questions:

Paul talks at length about boasting and compares his "pedigree" with his opponents' in order to discount their claims. When have you seen such comparisons within the church? What has been the effect?

Do Christians compete with each other to see who can be "holiest"? If so, what is the effect on the church?

Why would we as Christians be interested in placing ourselves above others, even in a spiritual matter?

Have you ever wished that you might be given the opportunity for a stronger spiritual experience in your life? If so, how might that experience help you to become a better Christian or prepare you to do greater work on behalf of Christ?

What do you do when life seems more like a series of "thorns in the flesh," than journeys into "the third heaven"?

What do you seek from God? What are you willing to do as Christ's follower?

Concluding the Lesson

▶ You may wish to offer the Scripture readings listed in the "Bible Background" for anyone wishing to do more study about ecstatic experiences or special revelations of God. Read 2 Corinthians 12:10 as a way of showing Paul's (and our) Christian goal.

Prayer

▶ Close with this prayer: "Gracious God, you have created marvelous and wonderful things beyond our knowledge. Continually surprise us by your Spirit and strengthen us for your Son's work in this world. Amen."

How Inclusive Should the Church Be?

Galatians 3:23-29

Purpose of the Lesson

The purpose of this lesson is to help adults understand inclusiveness as a valid model for all Christian congregations and to see where our own congregation may need to grow in that work.

Bible Background

The letter of Paul to the churches in Galatia is a freedom letter! He preached and taught the law and the relationship between faith and the law. Paul was born a Jew and lived the life of a faithful Jewish male. As he became a Christian and preached the gospel to non-Jewish persons, he understood that one came to righteousness and salvation by faith, not by keeping the Jewish law. Paul's Letter to the Galatians (and many of his other letters as well) became the foundation for Christian theology and helped to validate the presence of the Christian faith in a non-Jewish world.

The study book offers an explanation of the struggle Paul went through with the Jewish Christians in Galatia. What is important to realize is that as Paul called for a freedom in the new church's approach to the faith apart from Jewish law, he also became tremendously radical in his treatment of both women and slaves! In both the Gentile world and the Jewish world, women and slaves were without a doubt seen as second-or third-class persons and not really to be taken seriously in terms of faith. There may be exceptions, of course, but for the most part, women and slaves played only supportive or subordinate roles even within the church community.

Paul is often criticized for an apparent anti-female bias; but he clearly worked with women, such as Priscilla and Lydia, and acknowledged their ministry. He also had an intimate mentoring relationship with Onesimus, who was probably a runaway slave.

Perhaps Paul got carried away as he wrote the Letter to the Galatians, but it is a wonderful "carrying." He asserts that, within the baptism of Christ, and the faith that supports that baptism, men and women, Jews and Gentiles, slaves and free no longer can be or should be distinguished from one another in the church. Paul calls for oneness, for union, and for a complete equality in terms of one's faith relationship within the community of Christ.

For the church to benefit from this call to freedom, it may be beneficial to consider a simple description of different stages or forms of inclusivity. An early stage is tolerance. Persons from the majority and minority group hold to their own beliefs as right, or even as best, but make a conscious decision to assent, perhaps grudgingly, to the others' right to believe what they want and to be who they are. Tolerance presumes that "insiders" have to validate "outsiders."

A second stage may be acceptance, in which differences are overlooked or not noticed. Persons are regarded in their own right, but generally the majority makes and defines the rules. Values and visions begin with the majority mindset and are adapted, however cheerfully, for others. A more mature stage is inclusivity, in which the majority and minority are coworkers, cocreators, partners. The starting place for beliefs, values, behaviors, and decisions is still the majority group, but other groups are valued and sought out for their contributions. Beyond inclusivity is multiculturalism. When the cultures truly blend and class, race, gender, economic, and social barriers are removed, as in the body of Christ, all persons are valued as God made them. Beliefs, behaviors, and values are not predetermined or controlled by any one group.

Beginning the Lesson

▶ Ask the participants to divide into groups of three or four and to talk briefly about a time when they, or someone they know, were treated poorly or discriminated against simply because of their gender or their race.

Developing the Lesson

▶ Tell the group that Christianity offers a complete and reliable answer to discrimination, which we will explore today.

Words for Bible Times

▶ Review the material in this section in the study book. Explain the situation in the Galatian congregation. Give special attention to the issue of a blended congregation, in which both former Jews and Gentiles were working and worshiping together. Explain that, like most of the letters of Paul, the Letter to the Galatians is a vehicle for Paul, not only to encourage people in their faith development but to address controversy. Read Galatians 3:23-29 as Paul's response to the efforts of the Jewish Christians to force the Gentiles to follow Jewish law as well as the Christian faith. Ask:

How would you state in your own words the major themes of this Scripture selection?

If the Jewish and Gentile Christians were arguing about the "proper" way to come to Christianity, how might you have felt as a Gentile Christian in that argument? as a Jewish Christian?

What seemed to be at stake in the argument? (Possible answers: the Jewish Christians' heritage of Judaism, the foundation of much of their identity; assurance of the Jewish Christians of knowing how to approach religion and life; the threat of Gentile Christians having to come through a foreign set of rules and laws to worship God; loss of their religious freedom)

How might you have felt as a Gentile Christian after Paul wrote to clarify the relationship of church members to Christ and to each other? as a Jewish Christian?

Mention that most likely the letter would have been read to the congregation, perhaps by the one who delivered it. What do you expect was the reaction of the congregation members?

What do you think would have been the reaction to the references to women and to slaves?

Words for Our Time

▶ Review the "Bible Background" comments on tolerance, acceptance, inclusivity, and multiculturalism. Clarify terms so that you have a common understanding.

▶ Ask group members to think of any areas of your congregation's life in which someone either is particularly allowed or specifically denied access, even in subtle ways. Then ask:

Should there be any limits to the inclusiveness of our congregation? Explain.

What barriers are there in our congregation and/or in our denomination that inhibit inclusivity?

What, if anything, in Scripture, our church's tradition, or your own experience would validate a noninclusive stance? Explain.

▶ Pose the following scenarios, and ask the group members how they believe their church would react or respond. Ask them to consider these questions:

Would these persons be included, tolerated, or excluded? Why, do you think? What is the role of the church in their lives?

- Three families of another racial background begin to attend worship.
- A single parent with a live-in partner and children become regular attendees in this class.
- A white family of four visits and expresses interest in the church.
- A halfway house of criminal drug offenders calls the church to ask what time services are.
- A gay couple wishes to join the congregation.
- Two teenagers from a neighboring church want to join your youth group.
- A family with a child who has severe physical and mental challenges asks for him to be an acolyte.

Words for My Life

▶ Form groups of four or five persons. Keeping in mind the discussion on the scenarios, ask:

What is your responsibility as a Christian for working for and supporting an inclusive church?

What is your responsibility to model and to teach inclusivity?

Concluding the Lesson

▶ Read Galatians 3:26-29 again to the group.

Prayer

▶ Pray this prayer: "Give us the grace, O God, to live as the vessels of grace and love in this world. Forgive us, guide us, and encourage us, we pray. Amen."

What Is the Antichrist?

1 John 2:18-25

Purpose of the Lesson

The purpose of this lesson is to help adults explore the definition of *antichrist*.

Bible Background

A strong theme existed in both the early Christian church and in the Jewish faith during the time following Jesus' death and resurrection. Even the Qumran community of the Essenes had incorporated it into their beliefs. It was the idea of a battle to be waged between the "sons of light," or followers of God/Jesus Christ, and "sons of darkness," or those who would stand in opposition to God's will and salvation for the world or to the Jewish nation.

John was a strong Jewish Christian and wove the theme of light and darkness throughout his letter. The emphasis on the antichrist is one way of identifying those who have turned to darkness or who are now against God.

First John, probably written about A.D. 100, has a true sense of urgency about it. The letters of Paul, written at least a generation before, deal with matters of the faith, to be sure, but also confront more mundane issues as well, such as marriage and singleness, gluttony, and old habits of worship. John writes in an era in which the church was facing dangerous hostility from Rome. Nero (A.D. 37–68) had found in nearby Christians a convenient scapegoat for popular unrest. While his unwanted attentions were sporadic and confined mainly to Rome, his tactics were brutal. Memories of Nero's cruelty are prominent in the visions of the beast in the Book of Revelation. The emperor Domitian (81–96) was even worse, often inflicting hideous torture and death. Thousands of Christians were persecuted for their faith and many turned away or went into hiding. Christians accused anonymously were targeted as well. Under Nerva (96–98) and Trajan (98–117) Rome's policies moderated somewhat, but Christians who failed to recant their beliefs were punished, even martyred. Anonymous charges were ignored; still it was a hard time to believe in Christ.

It is in this era that John wrote his brief and urgent letter, which was very much to the point: "Hold fast to the truth of the gospel, and don't let others persuade you to move away from the light. The antichrist is strong and working against you, but God is stronger still." John is the only biblical writer to use the term *antichrist*, although other New Testament writers refer to the "lawless one" (Second Thessalonians), false prophets and false messiahs (Matthew and Mark), and beasts (Revelation) who were personified in a nation or individual opposed to God whom God would ultimately destroy.

John's notion of the antichrist, while not a human or superhuman being outside the faith community, is based on these figures. Someone is working to destroy the kingdom prepared by God. Those forces, suggest John, may be those anonymous (or even known) persons who have been intimately acquainted with Christians or Christianity and who now oppose them.

Christians were finding darkness in many quarters: the prevailing persecution of Rome, the myriad of false teachers and self-proclaimed messiahs, former believers who perverted the truth of the gospel, and heretics who preached contrary doctrine. John said in the midst of all this, "If what you heard from the beginning [the truth of Jesus Christ] abides in you, then you will abide in the Son and in the Father. And this is what he has promised us, eternal life" (2:24-25).

Beginning the Lesson

▶ Use the "Bible Background" and information from this segment of the study book to set the theme of John's letter. Ask participants if they have ever studied this letter in detail and if anyone can add any more to the information.

Developing the Lesson

▶ Tell the group that this session will clarify a "loaded" word in the Christian faith: *antichrist*. You will also consider those forces that work against Christ but were not specifically defined by John as the antichrist. Begin the session with a short prayer.

Words for Bible Times

▶ Ask someone to read 1 John 2:18-25. Invite the group to talk about the passage in general, and ask for their questions and comments. Note: some versions of the Bible, including *Today's English Version*, use the term *enemy of Christ* instead of *antichrist*. Be sure to use a version of the Bible (such as New Revised Standard Version) that includes the term *antichrist* in the first reading that the group will hear.

▶ Invite group members to place themselves in their imagination in the early church. Ask them:

How would you describe the antichrist?

What type of threat do you think an antichrist would have to the church?

How strong do you think the church was at that time? Help participants understand that the antichrists were those who used to be part of the church, but who had left the faith community.

How difficult would it have been in an early church congregation to cut off those persons from the fellowship and to consider their whole message and understanding of the truth to be a lie? Make sure participants understand that the church defined the antichrist as someone who intentionally and totally denied the faith and the truth of Jesus Christ as the Son of God.

Would you, as a member of the church, remain friends with someone who absolutely denied Christ? What about a family member?

What would it feel like to have to defend your faith and be threatened with losing your property, family, freedom and life by standing up against such antichrists?

Words for Our Time

▶ Have participants read this section of the study book; then ask them these discussion questions:

In contrast to the early church, the Christian church in the United States is pretty safe from the type of persecution suffered in the first century. Why is it that the church seems at times to be struggling to survive?

Is the antichrist (that is, a denial of Jesus Christ) present within the Christian faith today? (Possible responses may include mention of quasi-Christian cults, battles between Protestants and Catholics, serious disputes about doctrine that may be interpreted by some as heresy versus orthodoxy)

Some persons may interpret other religions as antichristian and their adherents as antichrists, especially when extremists kill or attack Christians. What is the Christian response to antichristian sentiment and actions? to antichristian violence?

Is the Gospel denied in our world? Explain. (Please try hard to focus the discussion on an honest evaluation of the place of the Christian faith in the world rather than on particular hot issues.)

How do the members of your church live out the gospel? How do you?

Does it make any difference to your community that your church exists? Explain as specifically as you can.

Words for My Life

▶ Form small groups of two or three persons, and ask them to talk with one another about ways in which they could strengthen their church and their own faith in a world that may not care what they believe or which stands against their faith.

Concluding the Lesson

▶ Remind the group members that the gift we leave each future generation is the gift of faith in Jesus Christ. Ask them to consider this week how well and how completely the gift is being given to the next generation.

Prayer

▶ Pray the Lord's Prayer as you close this session.

What Will Heaven Be Like?

Revelation 21:1-7

Purpose of the Lesson

The purpose of this lesson is to help adults study the images found in Revelation concerning heaven and earth, and to think about our own view of heaven and the eternal hope.

Bible Background

Many persons believe that the Book of Revelation is a book of prophecy that tells of the imminent end of the world. This perception has lingered from the time in the first century of the church when this book was written. Revelation, however, does not read or look like the prophecies of the Old Testament. The literary style of Revelation is apocalyptic, not prophetic.

Apocalyptic (meaning "revelation") literature is religious writing that offers hope and courage to the readers during a time of persecution or struggle. It is mysterious and veiled on purpose, with images that are hard to understand outside of the community for whom it was written. Both Revelation and Daniel are apocalyptic, being written during times of great struggle for both the Jewish and Christian communities. Dr. Bruce Metzger, in *Breaking the Code: Understanding the Book of Revelation* (Abingdon Press, 1991) does an excellent job of explaining the Book of Revelation. It is recommended to you for further study.

The Scripture for today's lesson may seem a bit unusual to us. John envisioned "a new heaven and a new earth; for the first heaven and the first earth had passed away" (21:1). At this end time, when God's holy reign would finally break through the bonds of sin that had held the world captive, the heavens (as a celestial creation) and the earth would be transformed into a new, Eden-like place. From the heavens would descend a new Jerusalem, which will be the ideal dwelling place of God and of God's creation.

For the early Christians and for the Jews, Jerusalem was truly the spiritual center of the universe. Although Rome was the center of the world's power, with the Empire headquartered there, Jerusalem was the place where God's presence was felt most strongly. The city was considered inviolable, since it was the chosen abode of God. But the city and the Temple were destroyed in 586 B.C., rebuilt, and destroyed again in A.D. 70.

Even to the Asia Minor churches who were the principal audience of John's Revelation, Jerusalem still was the holy place, the place of Christ's death and resurrection, of the Last Supper, of the ascension of Christ, of the Pentecost experience that brought the Holy Spirit and saw the beginning of the church. A divinely restored Jerusalem would attain a glory far beyond the earthly city, but would not need the Temple, because "the Lord God the Almighty and the Lamb" are the Temple (21:22).

This is the setting for "heaven," or what has been described in Lesson 14 as the kingdom of God. What will heaven be like? God will live among the people (21:3); there will be an end to sin (21:5, 8); the faithful will find transcendent joy (21:3) instead of the problems and limitations of physical life (21:4); and people will live in the perfect care of God, the perfect parent (21:7).

Beginning the Lesson

▶ Ask the group members for their ideas of heaven. Their ideas may include physical descriptions of things they have heard, or may simply be feelings that come to them when they hear about heaven. Write the responses on the chalkboard or on poster paper.

Developing the Lesson

▶ Tell participants that the descriptions about heaven come from different traditions in the church. Today, we will read what the Scripture says about heaven.

Words for Bible Times

▶ Invite a volunteer to read aloud Revelation 21:1-7 as the rest of the group follows along in their Bibles. Explain that John is recording his vision of heaven that occurs after the final Judgment and the reconciliation of the earth with Christ's second coming. Ask the group:

What does our Scripture say about the new heaven that is to

come? The Bible says very little or nothing about heaven, per se; John talks about the New Jerusalem as the place where God will dwell.

Why is it that we have such images in our corporate mind and memory about heaven, when this passage really talks about the New Jerusalem? Invite the group members to read Revelation 21:9-27, a description of the New Jerusalem, where humans will dwell eternally with God. Some persons interpret this vision literally and physically; others understand the imagery to reflect an intangible and perfected way of being.

What is the most important thing we may read about the New Jerusalem? (See 21:3, for example.)

What will the New Jerusalem be like?

What will be the quality of life there?

What does the description of this place sound like to you? Explain to the group that it sounds like heaven (also known to us as the kingdom of God or the kingdom of heaven), as God dwells with the people, and all sorrow and pain and hurt and fear and warfare is ended.

▶ Ask someone to read the last paragraph in this section of the study book beginning with "All this, as John saw it, comes after a universal and cosmic change."

Ask these questions:

As you imagine yourself as part of a persecuted congregation in Asia Minor, what do these words mean to you?

Knowing that Jerusalem had been destroyed by Rome in A.D. **70, and the Temple obliterated, does the idea of a new, eternal Jerusalem seem to be a dream come true? Why?**

How would that strengthen you for the persecutions that were to come?

Words for Our Time

▶ Form small groups of three or four persons and ask them to talk with each other about where on earth they have visited that seemed "heaven-like," (or "new-Jerusalem-like"). Use these discussion questions:

Is it really possible to create heaven ourselves in our own corners of the earth? If so, how? If not, what is missing?

Since Jesus Christ has already ushered in the kingdom of God, heaven is already here. What does this mean to you?

What responsibility does it place on all Christians? on you?

Words for My Life

▶ Ask the members in small groups to talk with one another

about one thing in their life that they wish could be changed to make it seem a bit more "heavenly." Have them next imagine just one day in which the pain and hurts and injustices of the world would disappear, and that we would simply be in the presence of God. Then ask:

With the promise of heaven waiting for us as Christians, what is it that allows us to live through our present days?

Why is that important as the followers of Christ?

Many of us imagine that we will be reunited in heaven with loved ones. What does the Scripture say about that?

Concluding the Lesson

▶ Ask the group members to think of one person they know who may need to hear the promise of the New Jerusalem. How might they share that news and hope with another person this week?

Prayer

▶ Close with this prayer: "O God, our help in ages past, our hope for years to come, be thou our guide while life shall last, and our eternal home; in Jesus' name. Amen."

To the Teacher

In TROUBLESOME BIBLE PASSAGES, VOLUME 2 we have included eight Scriptures from the Old Testament and fifteen from the New Testament and encourage you to take a fresh, new look at passages that may be familiar and unfamiliar to you at the same time.

How can the Holy Scriptures, which are a gift from God for our growth in grace and faith, be considered "troublesome"? These twenty-three passages may be called troublesome for one of several reasons: The Scripture

- appears to contradict other Scripture
- is problematic in its theological implications
- uses difficult language or uncommon imagery
- appears so lodged in its original cultural setting that it seems
- confusing or out of date for modern readers.

You may have heard these Scripture references many times; now they can come alive for you with insights and understanding that you never had before.

How to Use This Resource

Each passage is explained in its own context in the section "Words for Bible Times." Extra information is included in this leader's guide than appears in the study book. More contemporary approaches are considered in the section "Words for Our Time" and the personal touch for you is added in the section "Words for My Life." The teaching plan provides ways to study the Scripture from each of these three approaches.

In addition to the three main sections, there is an introductory exercise, "Beginning the Lesson," that helps study participants get their first glimpse of the session. In developing the lesson, start with the one or two overview ideas, and then expand the session according to the three major divisions. In the

"Developing the Lesson" section, each teaching suggestion is marked with an arrow ▶. Discussion questions are highlighted in bold type so that your eye is drawn to the proper place in the session plan. There are more than enough questions to focus and sustain an investigation into these passages.

Each session concludes with a summarizing activity and a prayer suggestion. We pray that your study of these Scriptures enriches your understanding and faith and leads you into a deeper relationship with Jesus Christ.

If You Like This Resource

If you enjoyed using *Troublesome Bible Passages, Volume 2*, you may want to consider the other volume in this series. Selected Scriptures are listed here so you can get a taste of what it offers.

Troublesome Bible Passages
8 sessions on the Old Testament
15 sessions on the New Testament

A Sampling:

Genesis 3:1-24	"Is All This Sinning Really Necessary?"
Exodus 20:1-17	"The Ten Commandments"
Job 1:13-22	"Why Do Innocents Suffer?"
Matthew 10:34-39	"The Radical Demands of Jesus"
Mark 13:1-37	"The End of Time"
Luke 13:1-17	"How Long Is God Willing to Wait?"
John 1:1-18	"The Word Made Flesh"
1 Corinthians 12:4-11; 14:1-19	"Speaking in Tongues"
1 John 4:1-6	"Testing the Spirits"

Troublesome Bible Passages is available from Abingdon at your local Christian bookstore.